Voicing God's Psalms

The CALVIN INSTITUTE OF CHRISTIAN WORSHIP LITURGICAL STUDIES Series, edited by John D. Witvliet, is designed to promote reflection on the history, theology, and practice of Christian worship and to stimulate worship renewal in Christian congregations. Contributions include writings by pastoral worship leaders from a wide range of communities and scholars from a wide range of disciplines. The ultimate goal of these contributions is to nurture worship practices that are spiritually vital and theologically rooted.

Published

Gather into One: Praying and Singing Globally
C. Michael Hawn

The Substance of Things Seen: Art, Faith, and the Christian Community
Robin M. Jensen

Wonderful Words of Life: Hymns in American Protestant History and Theology
Richard J. Mouw and Mark A. Noll, Editors

Discerning the Spirits:
A Guide to Thinking about Christian Worship Today
Cornelius Plantinga Jr. and Sue A. Rozeboom

Voicing God's Psalms
Calvin Seerveld

My Only Comfort: Death, Deliverance, and Discipleship
in the Music of Bach
Calvin R. Stapert

A More Profound Alleluia: Theology and Worship in Harmony
Leanne Van Dyk, Editor

Christian Worship in Reformed Churches Past and Present
Lukas Vischer, Editor

Voicing God's Psalms

CALVIN SEERVELD

William B. Eerdmans Publishing Company

Grand Rapids, Michigan / Cambridge, U.K.

Wm. B. Eerdmans Publishing Co.

255 Jefferson Ave. S.E., Grand Rapids, Michigan 49503 /
P.O. Box 163, Cambridge CB3 9PU U.K.

Printed in the United States of America

09 08 07 06 05   7 6 5 4 3 2 1

ISBN 0-8028-2806-X

www.eerdmans.com

For my incomparable wife, Ines,

and

trusty friend Barbara Carvill

Contents

Series Preface

Biblical Psalms

The Psalter of the Hebrew scriptures is the prayer book *par excellence* of the Christian church. Time and time again, worshiping communities have returned to the Psalter for inspiration and instruction in the life of prayer, both personal and public. Throughout the church's history, the most auspicious liturgical reform movements — including those of the sixth-century monastic communities, the sixteenth-century Lutherans and Calvinists, and the twentieth-century Liturgical Movement — have called for a renewed appreciation for the liturgical possibilities of the Psalter. If we want to understand better the DNA of the Christian faith and to deepen our worship, there is no better place to begin than with careful and prayerful engagement with the Psalms.

Yet the church has not always been a good steward of the Psalms as liturgical prayer. For one, we are often guilty of speaking the strange words of a lament or enthronement psalm without serious attempts to help worshipers have the slightest clue as to what they are saying. Here we might be helped by the advice of the Desert Father, John Cassian, that it might be "better for ten verses to be sung with understanding and thought than for a whole psalm to be poured forth in a bewildered mind" (*Institutions cenobitiques* [Paris: Editions du Cerf, 1965], II.xi, 76-79). For another, we often render the Psalms in remarkably unimaginative ways. Over three generations ago, theologian Earle Bennett Cross contended that "it is deplorable to waste the art and beauty of the Psalms on the desert air of systems of responsive readings which bore so many congregations to somnolence" (Earle Bennett Cross, *Modern Worship and the Psalter* [New York: Macmillan, 1932]). It is a critique that is as relevant today as then.

Thoughtful, prayerful use of the Psalms in both public worship and personal devotion requires theological poise, pastoral perception, and artistic imagination — all grounded as much as possible in the texts themselves. This volume is dedicated to nurturing these virtues.

Calvin Seerveld

Calvin Seerveld — philosopher, poet, preacher — is a lover of God and a careful student of the biblical text. Many of us who have been privileged to know him think of him as a kind of Jacob, as one who wrestles with God, seeking a blessing. Over the years, his curiosity and zeal have led him to wrestle not only with philosophers and modern artists but also with biblical accounts of or by Balaam and Balak, David and Asaph, Mary and Zechariah, all in the name and for the sake of Jesus Christ.

Even more significantly, Seerveld is a teacher. He is the kind of person who draws his students and hearers into deep engagement with texts. He models what kind of engagement with the Bible is necessary if we believe that God speaks through these texts. He demonstrates what it looks like to engage biblical texts with both heart and mind, passion and discipline. And he is willing to take the risk of using the kind of language that promises to convey the unvarnished truth of a text and evoke the kinds of affections that are equally true to the text.

I still recall the first time I sang his Advent hymn "O Christ, Come Back to Save Your Folk." A vivid text (though far from his most risky and adventuresome offerings), the hymn ends with the simple, direct, and lucid stanza: "O Christ! Remove our advent fears. Bolster our hope, excite our cheers. Bring on full life both new and free. Trumpet at last the jubilee." In a world of sometimes rather lackluster, comfortable worship, the church needs imperatives like "bolster" and "trumpet." They are words that grow in us new sensibilities, awaken in us new affections, and challenge us to new honesty and conviction.

The texts found here are similar. Seerveld's take on biblical Psalms and canticles is angular, rugged, vivid, and memorable. His offering helps us — even those of us living in the bland linguistic world shaped by writing for the Internet — approximate in English how angular, rugged, vivid, and memorable the original Hebrew actually is. And perhaps, by God's grace, these words will grow in all of us a deeper, more honest, more visceral faith.

Our hopes for this collection are threefold:

First, we hope that it will be a source of comfort, challenge, inspiration, and prophetic insight (even warning) for all who encounter it. These translations promise to be significant resources for personal, family, and group use in many settings. In particular, we hope that they will be a source of spiritual renewal for pastors, musicians, artists, and worship leaders who grow tired from the weekly pressures of leading others in prayer.

Second, we sense that several of these texts have great promise for use in worship. Their particular use will depend a great deal on the particular practices of a given congregation. Some communities, who thoughtfully limit public reading of scripture to authorized translations, may find here resources for prayers of praise, confession, lament, and thanksgiving. Other congregations may find particular texts here that will be read in worship in their entirety. Preachers and songwriters may find in this collection a word, phrase, or image to unsettle their thoughts about a given psalm and to suggest new angles for helping modern listeners engage the power of the text.

Third, we hope that this collection will be a catalyst for renewed creative engagement with these powerful poems. Seerveld stands in a three-thousand-year tradition of those who have edited, translated, adapted, and paraphrased these poems, as well as set them to music, especially with melodies for God's people to sing communally. We dare to hope that this collection might invite a new generation to stand in this venerable tradition. We hope it produces more Jacobs, more people who wrestle with God by wrestling with God's word.

We are also pleased to present the CD that accompanies this book. It contains recordings of several of these texts read by the author, along with several tunes that accompany the metrical settings found in the book. Additional tracks, as well as other complementary resources, can be found at *www.calvin.edu/worship/seerveld*. We hope that this recording will make its way into the cars and personal stereos of those with too little time to read, and to hospital and nursing home rooms of those unable to read. And we dare to hope that its compelling renderings of the text will lead a few more of us to slow down enough to give careful attention to the Word of the Lord. Thanks be to God.

JOHN D. WITVLIET
Calvin Institute of Christian Worship
Calvin College and
Calvin Theological Seminary

Acknowledgments

This book and CD presenting biblical psalms to be heard goes back a long way. Jon Pott, Editor-in-Chief at Eerdmans, first heard a few of the translations as a student in the chapel services of Trinity Christian College, Chicago, in 1959. My wife, Ines, shepherded our young family through fascinating sabbatical stays in Heidelberg, Munich, and Amsterdam in the 1960s and 1970s, allowing me to indulge my Bible-translating hobby. Emily Brink and ten dear persons of the Revision Committee of the Psalter Hymnal of the Christian Reformed Church (1977-1987) gave me an unstinting critical education in the versification of psalms and hymns — the best communion of the saints experience I have ever had. When I have been an occasional lay preacher during the past decades in Canada, congregations whose elders have come to trust me have allowed me to translate afresh the passage to be exposited on a Sunday, so I can continue to practice my craft to prick young ears to listen to the colorful accents of God's Word. And stalwart Barbara Carvill, colleague, mentor, and friend from the days when her husband, Robert, was still living, has quietly persisted in encouraging me to voice on tape a sample of my Bible translations.

After our son Luke made a demo tape, John Witvliet of the Calvin Institute for Christian Worship saw potential in its presentation for helping liturgetes and leaders who prepare worship services. I am deeply grateful for his taking up the project together with William B. Eerdmans to make it happen. Jon Pott, Jennifer Hoffman, and others at Eerdmans have given much valuable time and spirited supporting direction. Together, John Witvliet, Jon Pott, Jennifer Hoffman, Barbara Carvill, and Kristen Verhulst, with Emily Brink, have been a solid bank of counsel whom I could trust to modify (somewhat) my idiosyncrasies.

The pristine solo recorder playing by Cal Stapert of the Calvin College Music Department catches the haunting strength and intimacy of the Genevan and Welsh tunes employed for the various psalm versifications. Saxophonist Greg Marsden has sensitively performed the Blues lament of Psalms 56 and 92 as a suggestion of how believers can hew to the scriptural text yet make it newly heard. And Michael Page, with Calvin College students Lorien Reese, Dianna Clinch, and Noah Thomas, had the heart and mind and skill to embody and demonstrate the choral reading of psalms that an alert congregation can also do. The quality recording of Ed de Jong and Carl Hordyk assures me that these fallible translations of God's Word shall at least give a hint to those with ears to hear how we might bring the biblical psalms to vibrant life in our daily meditations and in our church worship services: a simple, sterling source of peace amid the troubles of our world.

CALVIN SEERVELD
Toronto
September 12, 2004

Introduction

God's psalms contained in the Older First Testament, as well as the "psalms" in the Second Newer Testament, are meant to be heard. For God's psalms to be heard, somebody must read them. To learn to read the biblical book of Psalms, one does well to realize that they are a collage of divine declamatory poems and not a simple prose series of human declarations. The biblical psalms have the LORD God talking through the embattled confessions of children adopted by God who are in the grip of God's Spirit. Yet, in the psalms, God is also talking live to anybody today, worldwide, who will listen.

Reading and hearing the biblical psalms

This book and CD together aim to help anyone who picks them up to start reading and listening to God talking live. Selected psalms from the canonical book of Psalms, but also psalmic passages from elsewhere in Holy Scripture, including the Newer Testament, are given in a fresh translation from the original Hebrew and Greek text. Some of them are also voiced aloud on the accompanying CD. To aid the reader's understanding of where to pause, the psalm texts are presented in their poetic, paragraphed nature (although the verses are noted for reference). Where the psalm calls for diverse voices or choral response to solo voice, that is also noted. One soon realizes that the psalms have a responsorial character: the speaker engages in a back-and-forth tussle with God, remonstrates with one's self, or actively talks to other saints or enemies nearby as if they were present.

The psalms can be attentively read in one's inner chamber, but even there the devotional experience of God's presence is heightened when one knows how to speak the text out loud. Readers are thus encouraged to read the text aloud. What the ear hears embodies what the eye sees. And once the text is voiced, God's Word is open to being heard by others. Since the biblical psalms originally were declaimed aloud, chanted responsively, and sung, we latter-day believers will miss the full richness of the psalms if we treat them only as script. Earlier believers also remembered God's songs with melodies running through their minds as they thought of the words (Psalm 42:4). It would be following a good biblical practice, then, to realize that the psalms were written not only to be heard but also to be sung. The church of our Lord has faithfully done that for centuries, until of late.

The peculiar rough and tender tenor of the biblical psalms

It is not easy today really to read and hear God's psalms as they are spoken and written, because we tend to cramp their poetry down to our own horizons. But we are called upon by God's Word to subject our expectations and prejudices to the warp and woof of God's biblical revelation so as to re-form and deepen our usual experiential assumptions. Our customary reading habits may be inadequate for hearing God speak through the psalms. The Semitic psalmists may seem extravagant to us proper Westernized believers and disbelievers. Is talking with God such an excitable life-or-death matter?

Deborah's song (Judges 5) vividly recounting bravery, killing, and cowardice is not for the fainthearted to sing. Hannah's psalm (I Samuel 2:1-10), which presages the Virgin Mary's exultant magnificat (Luke 1:46-55), grapples with the curse of abusive power and the LORD's deliverance of despised folk as only a Holy Spirit–filled woman could sense so well. The apostle James's hymn to Wisdom (James 3:13-18) does not blush to puncture the pretense of pseudo-wisdom by calling it "demonic." The apostle Paul's lists of concrete sin — wrangling, drug misuse, lust — and gifts of the Spirit — joy, kindness, peace (Galatians 5:16–6:2) — need to be heard like the poetic recitation of warriors' names in Homer's *Iliad* (II:494-877) or the roll call of foreign henchmen in King David's palace guard (II Samuel 23:8-39): a euphony of memorable sounds packed with a long history of specific, vivid meanings. Biblical psalmic passages are not sweet sentiments polished into British "heroic couplets," but sprawl with disciplined, rugged vigor. Biblical psalms in the Newer as well as in the Older Testament poetically concentrate passionate gritty insights into the crucible of a humble, offhand directness.

The Holy Spirit led certain persons to edit the book called Psalms into five sections (Psalms 1–41; 42–72; 73–89; 90–106; 107–150). Each section ends with a doxology. And no matter who the original writer was — David, Asaph (Psalms 50, 73–83), the sons and daughters of Heman in the guild of Korah (Psalms 42–49, 84–85, 87–88; I Chronicles 25:1-7), or an anonymous poet-composer — all the psalmists spoke as *chasidim* (the faithful ones) offering their *tehillim* (praise song) and *tephillim* (intercessory prayers) and *mizmor* (voiced melody) to the LORD God with uninhibited élan.

Therefore, anyone who picks up the psalms needs to realize a couple of things:

(1) The psalm writers act like children. Children can be naively outspoken in a way adults do not dare, because outspoken naiveté sounds self-indulgent, impolite, or over the top to us older folk. The psalmists seem by turn utterly crushed or downright audacious in their interchanges with God. The psalm writers can be so blunt as to admit to murder (Psalm 51:14) or to call God a "clothes-closet moth" (Psalm 39:11), because they blurt out things as faith-children and not as sophisticated skeptical adults or as believers who can pray sitting down.

(2) Every psalm writer-composer took for granted that he or she belonged to a peoplehood especially favored by God among the nations. And the psalmists knew experientially, despite their troubles, that they were at home in this world because the world was mercifully ordered by their LORD, the only true God. So the psalm writers had a certainty of God's holy presence and power that is hard for many of us to recapture in our artificially cluttered, often godless techno-culture.

These two points can help us later readers and speakers of the biblical psalms not to mishear them as the effusions of disgruntled, disbelieving complainers or of uncritical rah-rah cheerleaders. What the psalms reveal comes through the medium of Holy Spirit–breathed language born out of an impassioned, seasoned, educated faith that simply takes God at God's Word.

Linked thematic clusters of the biblical psalms

A person needs to develop a sense of the overall contents of the psalmbook so one can come to hear each psalm as one voice within the whole chorus.

What is presented here is a **pre-theological** book. The various psalms are gathered into clusters to give them a little context, and a couple of lines describe the content of each psalm to focus the reader's attention, but there are no arguments here to harness the psalms into certain theological dogmata to settle creedal disputes. God's original psalms are truly pre-denominationally ecumenical in their modeling a piety that the LORD will bless worldwide.

True, these psalms are read here as a chapter in the Bible of Jesus, because, as a Christian, I understand the Older and Newer Testaments to be intrinsically connected as God's directing Word for our historical lives here on the earth. The faith line of Abraham, Moses, David, Isaiah, and Jeremiah continues with the apostles, including Paul, to bring us the will of God and to show us the Ways to follow the Messiah, Jesus Christ, under the cloud and pillar of fire of the Holy Spirit.

It has gradually become apparent that Psalm 1 and Psalm 2 articulate concisely the worldwide vision and the ongoing mission in which God's Word of the psalmbook sets us to live and respond to God. Psalm 1 highlights the breath-taking *torah* of the LORD God as the horizon for orienting our vision of the world we inhabit. The LORD's **torah** (Section 1) gives us the lens through which to recognize that the created world belongs to God and is the good theater of historical operation for humans, animals, plants, rivers, and mountains for as long as God holds us creatures all together in existence.

Psalm 2 presents the human calling to act "in the order of **Melchizedek**" (Section 2). This unusual expression is the Older Testament way of saying that we humans are expected to rule God's world with a solicitousness and sacrificial care that are utterly selfless amid all the power struggles which terrorize history. The LORD God anoints us humans to mediate justice on the earth in the world which belongs to God until the Day of final reckoning.

Once one's consciousness is imprinted with the horizon of *torah* and Melchizedek as the sturdy, vibrant matrix of the biblical psalms, certain recurrent features throughout the collage of the psalmbook start to make terribly sound sense for today.

Although it is indeed God's world and it is our calling to be anointed believers "in the line of Melchizedek" — that is, to serve as mediating, peacemaking followers of the Christ (II Corinthians 5:17-20; Revelation 14:1-4) — there are also **enemies** (Section 3) afoot all around us whom we humans cannot help but face. The psalms explicitly face this fact. The world is not a rose garden without thorns, and evildoers and darkness plague our task of tending to the LORD's fields and vineyards. We are encouraged to lament the trouble in faith, but we cannot abdicate our responsibility.

Sometimes we who would serve the LORD of the harvest become ourselves enemies of God, sinners who waste what is good and violate our neighbors' lives (Matthew 20:1-16; 21:33-46). Basic to the world of the psalms is the reality that faith-committed persons in the order of Melchizedek need, at work and play under the LORD's *torah,* to **repent of sin and become forgiven sinners** (Section 4).

Given the ever-present threat of enemies and the reality of our sin and God's forgiveness, we come to the heart of the biblical psalms: **wrestle directly with the LORD in faith** (Section 5)! Go ahead! Don't be Pharisaically pious and add up your credits before God. Don't be Sadduceanly clever and try to find loopholes in the judgments against you. Take hold of God and pull on the LORD for a blessing! Do it with tenacious fear and trembling, as both that desperate deceiver Jacob and the ruined good man Job did once upon a time. The psalms are exercises in actually wrestling, in faith, with God in prayer.

Wrestling with God can preoccupy a man or a woman so much that the true horizons of God's compassionate *torah* and our official role as Melchizedek followers seem to fade from our sight. The **comfort** (Section 6) the psalms bring when they are truly heard is to remind us of the *torah* and the Melchizedek matrix determining our creatural existence.

Enemies and sin shall certainly someday be overcome. You can count on it, even if troubles continue!

When the sterling comfort of the psalms is heard, so you know that the LORD is firmly holding you and the whole world in God's hand, then **trusting God** (Section 7) like a little child kicks in again. Our hearts come to resonate with the covenantal faithfulness of the LORD, and we are strengthened to keep on going. The assurance of the **God-promises** (Section 8) in the psalms reinforces our Melchizedek-anointing and the blessed *torah* of the LORD by bringing a rainbow hope of fulfillment to creatures at large and the surety of ending our human temptation to sin. The explicit God-promise of peace, of shalom, activates our intercessory prayer for all those who struggle against evil and who seem unable to wrestle with God in faith.

A journey into and through the psalms ends with doxology. **Hallelujah!** by the faithful Melchizedek servants who are not found wanting (Luke 18:1-8) is in the offing (Section 9). Psalm praise is seasoned by tears but bursting with full-throated thanksgiving to the LORD who is acoming — soon! — to accept our grateful cheers. When, in a restored creation, it will always be an exuberant howdy, howdy, hallelujah! and never goodbye.

Good use of the psalm translations and versifications here presented

Translations of Holy Scripture are not innocent or timeless. Translators have dated locations, commitments, and limitations. The psalm translations printed here try to follow Martin Luther's policy of putting the original language texts into current, literate idiom — in this context American English.

Translations are not paraphrases. They hew to the original literary structure and historical strangeness more closely than giving the colloquial gist of the earlier formulation. A faithful translation of the psalms will plumb with restive intimacy the original **speakers'** message and try to catch the nuances in ways that still resonate today. A paraphrase formulates the conceptual point of the passage: a translation recapitulates the original tenor of the speaker, too, and lovingly converts its foreignness into a format that is accessible today but may also seem a touch quaint or unusual in the current tongue, so one catches a little of the otherness in what is being articulated anew.

On occasion in the translation here, I have supplied lines or phrases that are not directly implied in the original language text but I believe are consistent with the sense of the psalm. These are distinguished by being put in italic (the way the careful "King James" translators did it). A few key Hebrew terms like *mashiach, chesed, go'el* (or the synonyms for *torah* in Psalm 19) are also printed in italic in the text to remind us of the original language and to enlarge our vocabulary. I have done the same for the occasional Greek word. When I have inserted the original Hebrew or Greek word behind the translation, I have both printed the word in italic and enclosed it in brackets.

As noted earlier, some of the printed psalm translations here are voiced on the accompanying CD to encourage the reader, too, to read the psalms aloud. To voice a psalm is to be exegeting it. Reading a biblical psalm aloud is its aboriginal exposition, one might say, since **hearing** a psalm aright is primary. Because so much analytic explanation of the psalms discounts their defining "to-be-heard" quality, textbooks on the psalms tend to dry up or miss the convicting power of God's psalmic Word. You can have a tremendous critical knowledge of a psalm — its supposed original circumstantial employment, probable cultic use, and myriad facts about its Near Eastern parallels — but you have not come to **understand** the psalm unless you hear the merciful convicting call of the psalm to trust and obey God's specific Way for you and your neighbors in your present circumstances.

Some of the psalm translations here are followed by a complementary versification. These usually are fashioned to a Genevan melody from the 1500s or to a Welsh tune from more recent times, though I have also included two melodies from the German chorale tradition, a Basque carol, and two examples of the Blues. A psalm versification is a secondary exposition of its meaning, casting the psalm's proclamation into a regular stanzaic form that highlights the thrust of the psalm and accents its literary structure, key images, metaphors, and emphases, like refrains.

The versifications are not spoken on the CD but are meant to be followed while listening to the melodic line played on recorder or saxophone on the CD, which captures the tempo, rhythmic pulse, and color of the song and will help the listener to hear how the words could be meaningfully sung.

Genevan, Reformation German, and Welsh tunes are chosen because they seem to me to fit especially well the character of the psalms. God's psalms well up out of the troubled and jubilant lives of a believing peoplehood. So the German chorale format, which gave repeatable stanzas to the scriptural text rather than leave Bible verses in the episodic arabesques of Gregorian song which requires trained voices, put the psalms within reach of God's ordinary people. And Genevan and Welsh melodies have a sinewy, tough-love consistency to their longish lines that is most appropriate to the complexity of a psalm's conjunction of sorrow and joy. Such modal-sounding song is less familiar to our ears today which are attuned to major and minor chords, but Genevan lines are not intrinsically more difficult. John Calvin had the Genevan psalms learned first by the children so they could teach the adults! Psalms often need a rougher and tougher song line than the iambic pentameter and trimeter of Common Meter hymns from the 1700s, not to mention the prettified melodies and cadences of much contemporary praise music, simplified down from its revivalist American tent-meeting conception of faith-experience. Though composed in the past, these Genevan and Welsh melodies are in fact "new" in the double sense that to the rising generation they are mostly unknown and, as the Bible uses the term "new," are not worn out but still fresh, flexible, syncopatedly young, brimming with musical surprises.

Once we grow into the *torah*-Melchizedek vision and mission of God's Word in the psalmbook, and keep remembering the sweet parameters of confessing sin and occasionally not being able to restrain exclamations of "Yes, AMEN! Hallelujah!" — then we forgiven sinners shall be able to bask in the comfort of the LORD's God-promises and, even in the face of enemies, trust the Lord for blessing. To find comfort is not, of course, to be "comfortable." The psalms will always pinch your feet a bit, surprise your expectation, and twinkle your nose. That proves, as God's faithful listeners have always found, that God's psalms are eternally new, good news, for all occasions.

1 Torah

We are cradled as human creatures in God's
fantastic and ordered world.

Torah is the rich biblical term noted Jewish theologian Martin Buber translates *Weisung*, meaning the guidance and leading of the covenantal LORD God.

So *torah* refers to the marvelous creational ordinances of God which structure and set limits to the nature of creatural glory (Psalm 104; Psalm 148:5-6), like the amazing planetary orbits, the environmental metabolism of plants, the genetic code of animals, the normalcy of social structures like human tribes, families, and neighborhoods, and the various possible institutional forms for schooling, governing, and business. *Torah* refers also to the injunctions God gave in writing to Moses, like the ten "words" of instruction from Mount Sinai (Exodus 20:1-21; Deuteronomy 5:1–6:25) and the call to be pure and holy (Leviticus 19; Psalm 19:11-14). *Torah* includes the LORD's way of leading God's people historically out of their frequent punishing captivities (Psalms 78; 105; Romans 9–11).

Torah does not mean "laws" as a rigid set of prohibitions you are forbidden to transgress, a kind of club to knock you back into line (I John 5:3). The apostle Paul spent much time trying to disabuse legalistic Jewish and Christian believers of this one-sided negative conception of *torah* (Galatians 3–4; Romans 3:21–5:21). Even Jesus tried to free up the conservatist and liberalist leaders of God's people in his day from their small-minded restriction of God's will to statutes of cultic propriety and confessional piety by appealing to the cosmic ordinances God posited for the weather (Matthew 16:1-4; Luke 12:54-56)!

Simply put, *torah* refers to the underlying provident will of the trustworthy God of the universe and to God's Spirit-leading in the direction of shalom. *Torah* reveals creational laws like gravity to be God's hug for all creatures — not an impediment, but an upholding embrace. God's will reiterated at Sinai is a hedge to protect us from wasting our lifetime by stumbling off the Way of blessing. The LORD's *torah* reposited by Jesus Christ for us humans to follow (Matthew 5–7; Galatians 5:16–6:2) has the liberating effect of asking us to mature in thankfulness for the LORD God's loving hold on our daily lives and to bear each other's burdens. *Torah* is why Jesus taught us to pray, "Your will be done, O God, on earth as it is in heaven."

Psalm 1

Psalm 1 is a love letter from God, a beatitude. Blessed are the transplanted people: the women, men, and children who leave godless shenanigans behind and become rooted in the Ways of the LORD.

1   That man or woman is a happy one
    who does not practice the clever thought habits
        of godless people,
    who does not go stand around the way sinners do,
    or sit down with mocking, scoffing company.

2   *That man or woman is a happy one*
    whose pastime rather is the *torah* of the LORD,
    who ruminates on the *torah* of the LORD day and night.

3   That person is like a tree transplanted near running waters,
    a tree which bears its fruit on time
    and whose leaf does not wither —
    all that man or woman does is prospered!

4   It is not so with godless people.
    They are like chaff which the wind blows to bits.

5   That is why godless people
    — the sinners within the covenantal congregation too —
    that is why they cannot and shall not withstand Judgment:
    they are like chaff which the wind blows to bits.

6   The LORD God keeps close watch on the way of life the
        tried-and-true faithful lead:
  the way the wicked walk, however, shall end
        in permanent destruction.

Psalm 8

Psalm 8 celebrates the amazing LORD God whose creatures, like the stars and prowling animals, are astonishing wonders. And God makes us small humans to be lords over all these creatures. This psalm can be read antiphonally with voice chorus.

A melody by David for the attention of the music director,
using gittith stringed instruments

[Chorus begins]

1 LORD, our Lord! How wonderful is your name in all the earth!
   LORD, our Lord! How wonderful is your name in all the earth!
2 You who have set your glory in the heavens
     so that your adversaries, obstinate and vindictive enemies,
          may be stilled,
     you may now find that glory praised in the mouths
          of us babes and sucklings.

[Solo voice addresses God]

3 When I look at the night sky, the work of your finger,
   When I look at the moon and the stars, held there
          by your hand,
4 What are we mortal humans that you remember a man
          or a woman and pay them attention?

[Chorus thunders in answer]

5 You have made us humans almost like gods,
   crowning humanity with glory, a lordliness,
6 making us rule over the work of your hands,
   with everything put under our feet:
7 sheep and cows, wild animals of the fields,
8 birds of the heavens, fish in the waters
   and whatever other creatures prowl the deep paths of the sea —

9 O LORD, our Lord! How wonderful is your name
       in all the earth!
   LORD, *our Lord, how wonderful is your name in all the earth!*

Psalm 8 (Versification)

Lᴏʀᴅ God, how great your wonderful creation!
Your Name resounds through earth each generation.
Weak baby cries still celebrate your laws.
Your stunning deeds make even scoffers pause.

Amazed at night I scan the sky and linger
to see the moon and stars made by your finger.
What good are mortal humans on the earth?
Why do you gently care for us from birth?

Lᴏʀᴅ, you have made us humans truly lordly,
crowned us with cultivating might and glory.
Marvelous creatures — bird and fish and beast —
you have subjected underneath our feet.

Lᴏʀᴅ God, how great your wonderful creation!
Your Name is heard at large by every nation.
Grant us the grace and wise humility
to claim and serve your ruling majesty.

Tune: ɢᴇɴᴇᴠᴀɴ 8 (Genevan Psalter, 1551 edition)

Psalm 19

Psalm 19 declares the stunning *torah* of the LORD: creational order reveals God's merciful will for our lives. The glorious creatures at large are so many burning bushes of God's presence. For us to hear God speak in the tongues (*glossolalia*) of creation, we need a clean heart, waiting in awe for the LORD's voice.

A melody by David prepared for the music director

1 The heavens are telling the glory of God.
  The very shape of starry space makes news
        of God's handiwork.
2 One day is brimming over with talk [*'omer*] for the next day,
  and each night passes on intimate knowledge
        to the next night
3 — there is no speaking, no words at all,
  you can't hear their voice, but —
4 their glossolalia travels throughout the whole earth!
  their uttered noises carry to the end of inhabited land!

  God set up a tent for the sun at the ends of the earth —
5 have you seen the sun?! beaming forth like a bridegroom
        from his marriage-bed!
  The sun laughs joyfully like a strong man glad to run
        a race [*'orach*]:
6 it always rises from the edge of the heavens,
  and it circles over and around to the other ends of the sky —
  nothing is able to hide from its burning heat.

7 The leading [*tôrah*] of the LORD God is utterly reliable,
  bringing people back to life again!
  The magnificent testimonies [*'êdût*] of LORD God prove themselves
        to be everlastingly true,
  making inexperienced young people wise.
8 The commanding words [*piqqûd*] of the LORD God are
        truly straightening,

causing one's heart to laugh and be glad!
A task [*miswah*] imposed by Yahweh is bound to be
        integrally whole,
making one's eyes shine *with insight.*

9 Fear of the LORD God [*yir'at yhwh*] is cleansing:
it stands up forever and ever.
The ordering judgments [*mishpâtim*] of Yahweh are firmly
        true — Amen!
The LORD's fiats all together are thoroughly just

10 — more desirable than gold, yes, than much fine gold,
sweeter than honey, yes, than natural honey
        of the honeycomb.

11 Let me, your servant, also be warned by these ordinances, LORD,
for in keeping them much good results —

12 who can discern all one's errant missteps?!
O LORD! set me free from the spoilsome sins kept hidden
        from my notice!

13 And please hold me back from every overweening presumption
— I am your servant, LORD! —
Do not ever let self-confidence push me around:
then I will finally be able to be unpretentiously blameless,
rid of all the guilt-making rebelliousness. . . .

14 Let the sayings of my mouth and the inarticulate groanings
        of my heart
be something acceptable in front of your face,
O LORD God, my rock! the One who always comes through
        to set me free from my bondage!

Matthew 5

Matthew 5 offers God's benediction upon all those who listen to the Lord talk to them in their troubled daily life. God's good news frees men, women, and children from the curse of needing to master their destiny. The upside-down Rule of God in the world, following Jesus Christ, is simply to be merciful: *then* you are the salt of the earth!

1-2 When he saw the crowd of people, Jesus walked up the mountain a little way. After he sat down, his disciples came in closer. Then Jesus opened his mouth, as it were, and began teaching them these things:

3 The at-heart contrite ones are happy people,
because the Rule of heaven is theirs *for the asking.*
4 Men and women who are aggrieving are fortunate!
because they shall be comforted.

5 Blessed indeed are the gentle meek,
for they are the ones who get the earth as their possession!
6 Yes, those who are hungrily busy and thirstily waiting for the
righteousness of God to take hold
shall finally be completely satisfied!

7 Good for them to whom it is given to be merciful,
because their judgment shall be mercy itself!
8 Those who are truly innocent in their heart are happy people,
because they shall be able to look God in the eye.

9 And those who bring about genuine reconciliation among
men and women — good for them!
for they shall be given the special name, "Children of God"!
10 Yes, blessed are the ones who have been harassed and maltreated
because of their clinging to what is right to God,
because the Rule of heaven, I tell you, is theirs *for the asking!*

11-12 You are well off — I mean it! — when men reproach you, when women make it difficult for you, underhandedly gossip all kinds of misleading evil about you because you want what is right before me. When that happens, really be happy! laugh and be joyful! because God's compensation for you in heaven is truly great! (They did that, you know, relentlessly hunted down the prophets who were before you.)

13-16   So you are "the salt of the earth"!? Well, if salt freaks out flat, how will you ever get it salty again! It's not good for anything anymore, except to be thrown out and trampled on by people. You are "the light of the world" too, right? It's true, a city located on the top of a mountain cannot be put into hiding even for a minute; and you don't get a lamp lighted and set it under a little bushel basket, but you put it on a lampstand, and it shines for all those in the house. All right, let the light you have shine in front of people in such a way that they see the good work you do and come to praise your Father who is in heaven.

Galatians 5–6

Galatians 5–6 sums up how Jewish and Christian believers pervert God's *torah* by trusting solely in their self-reliant selves to win salvation by becoming law-abiding citizens. Until the Holy Spirit converts you into someone who actually is bearing your neighbors' burdens out of love for God, you have missed hearing and doing the will of the Lord updated in the *torah* of the Christ.

The apostle Paul writes:

5:16-18   What I am saying is this: carry out your daily walk led by the Spirit, and you will not gratify the desire of Sin. For Sin longs for the opposite of what the Spirit wants, and the Spirit sets its heart on what Sin detests: these two are antithetical to one another, so that you do not do what you would really like to do. But if you are led by the Spirit, you are not stuck under the law.

19-21   It is obvious what the deeds of Sin are: whatever works immorality, impurity, shameless lust, idolatry, getting high on drugs [*pharmakeia*], hateful hostility, wrangling, factional rivalry, outbursts of anger, ambitiousness, dissensions, sectarianism, envy, drunkenness, all-night carousing, and such stuff — I want to tell you plainly, as I warned you before, that those who are busy doing such things shall not inherit the kingdom of God.

22-24   But the fruit of the Spirit is intense love, joy, genuine peace, long-suffering, kindness, upright goodness, faithfulness, gentleness, self-control — against such fruit there is no law! And those who belong to Jesus Christ have crucified the Sinful with its kind of passions and desires.

25-26   Since we live by the Spirit *in our hearts,* let us also actually walk by the Spirit. Do not let us become eager for empty glory, irritating one another, envying one another.

6:1-2   Brothers and sisters, if a man or woman is detected in some misdeed, you who are Spirit-filled, help bring such a person back to the right way in a spirit of gentleness, looking out for yourself that you not be tempted too. Keep on bearing each other's burdens, and in that concrete way you will be fulfilling the law of Christ.

2 Melchizedek

Our daily life happens sadly amid a rough tumble
of public historical struggles in front of God's face.

Melchizedek is not a familiar name today. There are not yet **MELCHIZE-DEK** T-shirts for sale in Christian bookstores.

The original Melchizedek ("king of right-doing") is the mysterious figure who blessed Abram after Uncle Abram's armed men rescued nephew Lot from the kings who had pillaged Sodom and Gomorrah. Melchizedek gave Abram a high-priestly blessing in the name of the Most High God (Genesis 14) just before Yahweh covenanted with Abram, who was then renamed Abraham, to bless the whole world through his obedient descendants (Genesis 12:1-3; 22:15-18; Galatians 3:1-14).

Also, King David was inaugurated as a priestly king "in the order of Melchizedek" (Psalms 2:4-9; 110:1-3), since David was anointed by the LORD to bring compassionate just-doing to God's people and Jerusalem so that the city could rightly be called "the city of God" (I Samuel 16:1-13; II Samuel 6–7; Psalms 46:4-6; 48).

The Letter to the Hebrews in the Newer Testament takes great pains to identify Jesus Christ as a God-man "Melchizedek" mediator whose regime brings to an end once and for all the need for us men and women to sacrifice things to make good for our sins and certifies that the ministry of Christ's followers be only one of thankful right-doing (Hebrews 4:14–10:39).

So "Melchizedek" stands for the mysterious mediating role of men and women who are anointed by the LORD God to rule and lead others with, as it were, their slip of mercy showing. The Melchizedek dynamic pervading the psalms is the call of the LORD, within the secure framework of God's cosmic *torah,* for us humans to be busy as redemptive rulers over what happens day by day in society. As Jesus Christ, the Messiah, was anointed to mediate reconciliation between sinners and the LORD God, so followers of the Christ, in the knightly order of Melchizedek, are anointed to be *tsaddiqim* (right-doing ones) who bring compassionate just-doing into the public square. *Tsaddiqim* will govern with mercy, because these right-doing ones are not ensnared in the partisan mania of some idol (Psalm 115:3-8) and are utterly certain that the LORD shall in time pick up the broken pieces of our lives (Ecclesiastes 3:1-15). Melchizedek rulers minister to others with a gentleness peculiar to wisdom (James 3:13-18).

Melchizedek, then, is the biblical code name for being an ambassador on earth for God revealed in Jesus Christ, to bring healing to the nations of the world (Deuteronomy 28; Isaiah 60–62; II Corinthians 5:17-21). Melchizedek is why Jesus taught us to pray, "Lord, may your kingdom, your Way of ruling, come . . . soon."

Psalm 2

Psalm 2 faces us with the historical reality of power politics. Yet the Lᴏʀᴅ God laughs at every Nebuchadnezzar and Herod who vaunts his cruel domination. The Lᴏʀᴅ promises that those whom God anoints will be safe from the Evil principalities which beset us. Whoever follows the Anointed Messiah, the Christ, will find shelter. This psalm can be read as a choral reading in a worship service.

The wise cantor:

1 Why do the peoples of the world rage about like madmen?
  Why in the world do the different nations keep on
        thinking up stupid schemes?
2 Earth kings get together "for a consultation" —
  important rulers hold conferences all together
  against the Lᴏʀᴅ God and against God's anointed one *(mashiach)*.
  These earthly rulers say:
3 "Let us smash the chains of this God that hold us down!
  Let us throw off the reins of God's 'anointed one'!"

Another liturgete, perhaps a priest:

4 The One who sits enthroned in heaven begins to laugh,
  my Lᴏʀᴅ mimics their foolish bluster;
5 and then God turns to them in holy anger,
  stops the upstarts short with God's fierce outrage:
6 "It was I! it is I who have set up my anointed king
  on Zion, my set-apart mountain."

Princely ruler taking official part in the liturgy:

7 Yes, I will recite the decisive appointment by the Lᴏʀᴅ God.
  God said to me:
  "You are my son. Today is the day I have borne you.

8 Ask it of me and I will give you peoples of the world
         for your heritage;
   the most distant nations of the earth will be yours to tend.
9 You may have to break them with a rod of iron.
   You may have to smash them for remolding
   as a sculpting potter reshapes her clay dish —"

[The congregation stands]

Wise cantor again:

10 So now, you small-time little rulers, you had better wise up!
    You who only judge on the earth,
    hadn't you better get the point?
11 Serve the LORD God with an attentive awe —
    Take joy *in your task only* with trembling —
    Give homage to this *adopted* son *of God too* —
    lest he also get worked up, and you obliterate any way
         for you to walk,
    for God's anger can flash up like lightning. . . .

Congregated chorus:

12 Blessèd are all those who have run
    to take shelter with the anointed one.
    Blessèd are all those who have run
    to take shelter with the anointed one.
    Blessèd are all those who have run
    to take shelter with the anointed one.

Psalm 2 (Versification)

Why do the nations rage and plot for war?
though all their schemes for ruthless power are thwarted?
Earth's mighty rulers boast against the LORD:
"We shall remove the bonds of God's anointed."
God sits in heaven, laughs them to derision.
My LORD in anger says what God has done:
"I place in Zion one with holy vision
who shall do justice so my kingdom come."

God firmly told me: "You are my own son —
to lead all people you have been begotten.
Subdue and reconcile to me each one,
though they be smashed like vessels of a potter."
Therefore, you worldly rulers of the nations,
judge in the LORD's way, tremble to be just.
Fear godly anger if you break God's patience:
but safe are those who serve the LORD in trust.

Tune: GENEVAN 2 (Genevan Psalter, 1539 edition)

Psalm 110

Psalm 110 is the psalm most quoted in the Newer Testament: God is going to reduce the enemies of the Lord to footstools for God's anointed ones! The LORD God calls us to a Melchizedek leadership in the world: be a *priestly* ruler — set things right as a mediator who reconciles justly, though it cost you your life.

A melody by David

1 This is what the LORD God says to my Lord:
   "Sit at my right hand
   until I have put down your enemies
   as a footstool for your feet."

2 The LORD God will give free rein to the official scepter
            of your power.
   Go ahead, rule from Zion in the thick of your enemies!
3 On your D-day your folk will be willingness itself,
   wrapped in the splendors of consecration.
   Just as dew springs from the womb of sunrise,
   so shall your youthful strength surprise you.
4 *I repeat, David,* this is what the LORD God has sworn,
   and God will not have second thoughts about it:
   "Henceforth you are a priest forever
   in the order of Melchizedek!"

5 My Lord is at your right hand, *people.*
   My Lord shall break kings to pieces in the day of his anger.
6 My Lord shall set things straight in the nations filled
            with corpses.
   My Lord shall shatter those who are head over most of the earth —
7 *God's anointed one* shall be able to drink water from the
            running stream
   nearby the way *of judgment:*
   that is why God's anointed one shall be able to hold head up high!

Psalm 110 (Versification)

"Sit at my right hand," said the LORD to my Lord,
"while I subject your foes beneath your feet."
The LORD shall bless your ruling from Mount Zion
— right in the thick of enemy deceit.

Your youthful strength shall come like dew at sunrise
to lead your pledged folk ready for the fight.
The LORD has sworn, God never shall revoke it:
"You are a priest-king called to acts of right."

The sovereign Lord stands guard for your protection;
he shall wreak vengeance on the Judgment Day.
The Lord shall smash all military forces
which proudly feast-kill, waste the meek as prey.

The LORD makes covenant with God's anointed
who follow Christ, the true Melchizedek:
daunted in struggle, you shall drink fresh water,
and hold your heads high, safe as God's elect.

Tune: GENEVAN 110 (Genevan Psalter, 1551 edition)

Psalm 115

Psalm 115 was Jewish theologian Martin Buber's favorite psalm. Like Isaiah in chapter 44, the psalmist here mocks those who worship idols, because such people become impotent and destructive like the false gods they serve. The true LORD God, however, is a sure relief and a protection for God's folk who trustingly tend the earth while they live. The rendering below is for communal responsive reading aloud.

Leader: Not for us, LORD, not for us,   1
        but do something glorious for your name!
        Make something solid and shining to show your
        covenanting Grace and utterly dependable faithfulness!
        Why should the peoples all around say,

        "And where now is their God"?   2

People: **Our God is in heaven!**
        Everything that pleases God, God completes!   3

Leader: Their "gods" are solid gold and silver,   4
        but made by a human hand.
        Their fake gods have a mouth but cannot speak;   5
        they have eyes but cannot see!
        Ears they have but cannot hear;
        a nose is there, but they cannot smell —   6
        Their hands cannot touch things.
        Their feet cannot go for a walk.   7
        No sound passes through their throat. . . .

People: **Like them become those who made them!**
        Like them become all those who feel secure
            with them.   8

Leader: Israel! get to feel secure with the LORD God: 9

People:	**a relief and a protection is the LORD for such people.**
Leader:	Priestly house of Aaron! bind yourselves only to
	the LORD God: 10
People:	**a relief and a protection is the LORD for such people.**
Leader:	You *newcomers* who fear Yahweh! trust — trust
	the LORD God: 11
People:	**a relief and a protection is God for such people.**

Leader:	The LORD God has kept us in mind: God shall bless —	12

People:	**Bless the house of Israel!**
	Bless the priestly house of Aaron!
	Bless those who fear the LORD GOD!
Leader:	— the unimportant ones together with the very
	important ones. . . . 13

May the LORD God prosper you, you and your children.   14
May you all be blessed by the LORD God,
who made heaven and earth.   15

Heaven, you know, belongs specially to the LORD: 16
The earth is what God gave for the sons and daughters
    of man to tend.
Dead men and women do not praise the LORD,   17
not one of those who have gone down to where it is
    deathly still.
But we people here, let us praise the LORD!   18
from now on and for evermore:

People:	**thank God — hallelujah!**

Ecclesiastes 3

Ecclesiastes 3 lets us confront the question of "What in God's hurly-burly world does anything mean anyhow, if there is a time for all matters under the sun, which seem to cancel each other out?" The mysterious, comforting faith response we are asked to hear is this: "God picks up the broken pieces."

1 Is there a right time for everything?
There seems to be time for every kind of activity under the sun:
time to be born and time to die,
time for planting, time for weeding out what was planted,
3 a time to kill and a time to heal,
time to break down and time to build up,
4 time to weep and time to laugh,
a time of mourning, and a time of dancing around,
5 time to throw stones and time to pick up stones,
a time for embracing and a time to keep yourself far away
    from embracing;

There seems to be
6 a time to struggle for something and a time to give it up as lost,
time to save things and time to throw away things,
7 time to tear things to pieces and time to sew things together,
a time to keep quiet and a time to speak out,
8 time to love, time to hate,
a time of close in-fighting and a time of being at peace. . . .

9 What's the use?
What is left over of the labor to which a man or woman
    exerts oneself?

10 I have come to understand this miserable problem which God
    has given to human creatures to bother them.
11 Everything God has ever done is very good, beautiful, done
    at the right time.

This timing, eternity, God has put at the heart of man
      and woman too
(this does not mean a human creature can find out what God
      actually has done from beginning to end).

12 I have come to understand that a human can do nothing
      good oneself,
that for a man or woman to be glad, to be well-off,

13 even to be able to eat and drink and enjoy oneself in the press
      and change of daily life —
all this is purely a gift of God.

14 And I have come to understand that whatever God does
      lasts forever —
nothing can be added to it and nothing can be taken away
      from it.
God has set things up this way so men and women will fear God.

15 Whatever is and will be has already been: **God picks up
      the pieces.**

James 3

James 3 probes the heart of our human deeds, which are so often double-minded, two-faced, underhanded, or blunt as hell. True wisdom is not partisan, ambitious, and outspoken so much as firmly conciliatory, empathetic to the other person's needs, and full of good will. Evil "wisdom" is suspicious, calculating, and harsh: godly wisdom is without guile, carries gentleness in its ruling, and brings hope.

13   Is there a wise man or woman among you? one who knows surely what he or she is doing? All right, let that person show it by their daily deeds, dealing wholesomely with others in a gentleness peculiar to wisdom.

14-16   But if you have ruthless contentiousness and ambitious rivalry in your hearts, do not boast *about* your *"wisdom,"* do not lie against the truth. Such "wisdom" has not come down from heaven: it is utterly earthbound, emotionalistic, demonic. Wherever jealous envy and selfish ambition exist, there you will always find upheaval and every kind of mean skullduggery.

17   Wisdom from heaven is first of all worshipful; it also engenders peace. True wisdom is willing to wait, is able to be talked to, is full of mercy and good fruits, not uncertain, but unhypocritically open-whole-hearted.

18   The fruit of doing what is right before God is sowed by peacemakers in that peaceable spirit of rich wholesomeness.

3 Enemies

Entreating God for help against implacable enemies can teach us to voice unashamed expectation of rescue.

Enemies, as the psalms understand them, do not go out of date or run away; they are always hanging around. But biblical enemies are not just nasty people who make life miserable for you and for others. Enemies in the psalmbook are enemies of **God**, hostile forces that try everywhere to lay waste the beginnings of the "shalom" God provides in history.

Prototypical enemies are disease and death, drought, floods and plagues, devils, and any systemic form of godless violence that works to destroy life on earth. The special enemy that is inscrutable Evil has the monstrous character of chthonic principalities and powers loose in God's world. These powers remain beyond the ken of us humans but wickedly attack us mortals, often by the hand and tongue of Evil-doers who deceive, murder, abuse, rape, or kill innocents, even by sins of omission. Well-intentioned people of God like Job's self-righteous "friends," as well as the profligate sons of respected cleric Eli (I Samuel 2:12), can become enemies of the Lord too.

All destructive forces and their henchmen can be railed against in faith as enemies, because such usurpers of God's will for creatures do not belong in God's world and are due to be purged. Enemies — within the covenanted communion too (Psalm 1:5) — foolishly try to disrupt the Lord's *torah* and aim to thwart the grace served in the order of Melchizedek by dragging people back into the slavery of self-reliance.

Faithful followers of Christ in the knightly order of Melchizedek, however, do not fight the fire of the Dragon with fire. The weapons of God's wounded people against enemies are the sword of the Spirit and the powerful Word of God (Ephesians 5:16-23). So the psalmists lament the enemies whose unbridled power ruins the *magnalia Dei* and cripples God's people and their neighbors.

In the face of enemies, the psalmists' laments of faith are cries of pain which by the very act of lamenting bring a measure of healing, because they voice a certain kind of hope which verily expects God to cut short the Lord's apparent inactivity in tending to the helpless. And the severe lamenting curses in the psalms are intercessory prayers made *in extremis* by faith-dependent children of the Lord who cannot cope with the Enemies' overpowering harm to them; so they helplessly cry out to God for **God** to exact judgment on the ruthless and to rescue the weak (Psalm 137:7-9; Philippians 4:4-7).

The psalm awareness of enemies helps us know what the historical reality actually is: Satan's cohorts are in retreat but with seductively undermining or threatening slash-and-burn tactics in operation (Luke 10:17-20; John 12:27-31; 16:1-11; Revelation 12). Taking enemies "psalm-seriously" gives grit to one's daily prayers. No wonder Jesus taught us to pray, "Deliver us from the evil one," God's protean adversary.

Psalm 3

Psalm 3 encourages any beleaguered believer to ask God to rough up the enemies who are out to hurt God's people. The LORD is an umbrella over those who expect God to protect them.

A song to be sung, composed by David around the time when he was
trying to get away from his son Absalom, who was hunting him down

1   LORD God, there are so many people after me!
    A mass of people have set themselves up against me.
2   So many people are saying to me,
    "There is no rescue for you with God!"
3   But you, LORD God, are like an umbrella over me.
    You are what distinguishes me! holding my head up high.

4   I cry out my loud cry to the LORD God,
    and God answers me from God's holy mountain.
5   When I lay me down to sleep I do wake up again,
    because the LORD God supports my waking.
6   I will not be afraid of an army of ten thousand people
    who set themselves up against me, surround me —

7   Get up, LORD God! Rescue me, O my God!
    Yes, you can break the jaw of all my enemies.
    You smash the teeth of those who are crooked!

Congregated faithful:

8   Rescue — deliverance — **does** belong to the LORD God!
    May your blessing, LORD, rest upon your people.

Psalm 5

Psalm 5 is an embattled call for God to frustrate the smooth-talking deceivers who mislead people around you. The LORD's grace, like a great big shield, will indeed surround anyone who truly loves God.

A tune by David for recorders and the music director

1 Make your ears open, O LORD, for what I have to say!
   Would you please try to understand how bothered I am?
2 Pay attention to my "Help!" cry —
   You are my king! my God! It is to **you** I make my appeal!
3 O LORD! hear my voice in the morning —
   this morning I'll just spill it out to you
   and then get set to see what happens. . . .

4 For you are not a God, are you, who can put up with what is
            not just!
   Whoever undermines things, you cannot stomach, right?!
5 People who push themselves forward shall never be able
            to stand their ground in front of your eyes, O my God!
   You hate — I know that — hate all those who work out what
            is deceptive!
6 You will utterly ruin those whose talk misleads!
   Men with gossiping blood on their hands, the tricky ones,
            make you, O LORD God, vomit!

7 But in spite of them, because of your overwhelming
            promising mercy,
   I am come to the place where you are;
   I am humbling myself right near your specially consecrated
            temple, awestruck before you.
8 O LORD! lead me in your kind of doing what is right,
   especially because of those just waiting to find out where
            my weak spots be! —
   please lay your path straight out in front of me. . . .

9 For there is absolutely nothing that comes out of their mouths
        you can count on!
    What's inside them causes rot!
    Their throat is like a grave ready to swallow!
    They just keep on sucking you in with their slippery tongue.
10 O God, make them pay for it!
    Let them get caught and smashed by their own devious plans!
    Fragment them to pieces because of their many, many
        underhanded deeds!
    For it is against **you** they are breaking things down —

11 But let everybody who really trusts in you be glad;
    let those who try to hide themselves in you be able to laugh
        joyfully again and again forever!
    Cover them protectively, Lord, so that they may indeed relax
        happily with you,
12 those who really love your Name;
    for you are the One, O Lord God, blessing the man and woman
        who does what proves true.
    You surround them with grace, like a great big shield. . . .

Psalm 22

Psalm 22 contains the anguished cry Christ quoted on the cross: "My God, O my God, why have you left me in the lurch? You cared for me as a baby and have always saved my forebears. Lowering evil persons are set to make mincemeat of me — I'm scared to death! Hurry up! Help me!" And the last paragraph of Psalm 22 — which Christ also knew ended the psalm — thanks the LORD for coming through with rescue: so I'll hallelu the LORD right here among the congregated faithful!

A psalm of David for the director of music, to be sung
to the melody of "Red deer in the red morning light"

1 My God, my God, why have you left me in the lurch?
   Why do you hang back from helping me?
   Why are you deaf to my weeping?
2 My God, I call out to you day and night, I don't stop,
            and you don't answer me!
3 You are the Holy One, aren't you? the one who receives
            the praises of Israel?

4 Our forefathers and mothers trusted you, they trusted — and
            you helped them!
5 When they cried out to you, they were saved!
   They trusted you and were not left shamefaced. . . .

6 Am I a worm and not a man!?
   the laughingstock of people, something to be jeered and
            trampled on?
7 Everybody who sees me pokes fun!
   They curl back their lips, shake their heads, and sneer:
8 "Truckle over to the LORD God, maybe God will help you!
   Sure — God'll save you, because you are 'the apple of God's eye'!"
9 Yes, O God, you are the One who lifted me out of my mother's
            body, who made me feel secure at my mother's breast;

10 I have always toddled over to you since I was born. . . .
   You have been my God from my mother's womb on —
11 Don't go away from me now!
   For the terrible Darkness is coming,
   and there's nobody around to help. . . .

12 Great big bulls surround me.
13 And huge beasts from far away are circling in, jaws open
            like pawing, bellowing lions!
14 I feel like water all shook up;
   my bones seem to be disintegrating;
   my heart has melted like a piece of wax somewhere inside me;
15 my throat is terribly dry; my tongue is stuck to my mouth —
   are you going to put me in the dust of death?
16 Because those huge dogs are all around me,
   the whole dirty crowd of cutthroats are coming in for the kill:
   they're going to tie me up hand and foot!
17 I can feel every bone —
   Look! They are looking me over, looking me all over;
18 I know, they'll take off my clothes and throw dice to see
            who gets it —
19 O Lord God! Don't you go away from me . . .
   Almighty One! Hurry! and help me!
20 Save me from the cut of death!
   Spare me from those voracious dogs!
21 Protect me from the lion jaws!
   Snatch me away from those horns of the bulls!

22 I will proclaim your name, O Lord, to those close to me.
   I shall shout out "Hallelujah" right in the middle of
            the congregation:
23 Hallelujah! Hallelujah! All here who fear the Lord!
   Praise God! all children of Jacob!
   Stand in awe of God! all tribes of Israel!

24 For the LORD God has not deserted,
   the LORD God has not left me, a man of deep sorrows,
      has not left me in the lurch —
   The LORD God has not hidden God's face from me but has heard,
   because I cried out to the LORD!

25 Thank you, LORD, that I may sing this psalm before all the
      people this morning.
   Thank you, LORD, that I might fulfill my vows before those
      who fear the LORD.

26 And someday all poor, miserable people will eat together and
      be happy —
   the LORD God will "Hallelu" those who have searched for God —
   and they shall live on richly together forever and ever.
27 And someday all the ends of the earth will know and turn
      to the LORD —
   every kind of people will fall down at your foot, [O God] —
28 because Power is the LORD's!
   God rules the nations of the world.
29 And someday all asleep in the earth, yes, everyone turned
      to dust,
   will have to humble himself or herself, tremble, before the face
      of the LORD.

30 My generation will work hard for the LORD;
   the coming generation will be told of the LORD God,
31 and they shall testify of this God's faithfulness to generations
      still not born —
   because the LORD God has saved me.

Psalm 22 (Versification)

My God! O my God! Have you left me alone?
Why have you forsaken me, deaf to my groan?
I cry to you daily and plead late at night,
but you do not answer or pity my plight.

Yet you are the Holy One, Israel's King,
to whom all our fathers and mothers did sing.
They counted on you to come through when they prayed;
whenever they trusted, then you always saved.

Yet I am a worm who is laughed at and mocked,
despised by the godless who saunter about.
"His help is the LORD! Foolish fellow," they sneer,
"let God set him free since God counts him so dear."

Since I was a baby, dependent and weak,
I nestled in safety, LORD, close to your cheek.
Please don't go away, for deep trouble is near!
Who else can secure me and keep away fear?

Surrounding brute beasts make me shudder with fright,
and jaws of fierce lions are ready to bite.
My bones seem disjointed, I can't catch my breath —
my heart melts like wax, and I face cruel death.

Like dogs they surround me, I cringe and I groan;
they pierce through my hands and my feet to the bone.
They measure me out for the kill, as they gloat.
They scatter their dice for my garments and coat.

My God! O my God! Do not leave me exposed.
Voracious, these dogs only deepen my woes.

These beasts, mad with violence, want me to die:
O stop them, Almighty, and answer my cry!

I shout out your praise to your saints who endure.
Praise God, all you faithful: God's comfort is sure!
The LORD has not left me or hidden God's face;
I cried out for help, and God saved me in grace.

Those hungry for fullness will feast with the LORD.
All peoples will worship the God they ignored.
Yes, even the proud will be humbled in dust
to honor God's power — the LORD whom we trust!

I thank you, my LORD, I may sing with your folk
to seal here in worship the vows which I spoke,
so new generations shall pass on in faith
that you, O my God, keep your children all safe!

Tune: MALDWYN (1600s, Welsh)

Job 19

Job 19 bodies forth the extraordinary testimony of Job at his wits' end because of his undeserved suffering and the stupid, pompous judgments of his "friends": "I know for certain, that even if the worms get to eat my body, I shall see God! I will see God myself, and God will not be an opposing stranger to me!"

1   Then Job began his answer:

2   Just how long are you going to keep on needling me deep inside
            where it hurts?
    trying to batter me to pieces with your empty, empty! words?
3   You have twisted things to make me look bad again and again —
            isn't it enough now!
    It doesn't shame you in the least, does it? that you do me in!

4   Suppose — O.K. — suppose I have unconsciously sinned.
    Suppose there is a blind spot, some wrong thing I happened
            to do:
5   so you make a big deal out of it! — is that what you are after?
    You are going to set me straight by rubbing my face in it!?
6   You had better realize it is God who is the One that is
            crimping my life.
    God has tangled me up all around in God's net!

7   Don't you see that?
    My plaintive cry keeps on going out, "I am being wronged!"
    but I get no answer.
    I plead, crying for help, but there is simply no justice done at all!
8   God has blocked off my path, and I cannot go on further!
    God has shrouded the way I am walking with deep darkness!
9   Any honor I once had, like clothes God has stripped off of me.
    God has removed the respect I once bore.
10 God has leveled me this way and that way and the next way
            so that I am in ruins!

Even my hope God has rooted out and blown away like a tree
  in a tornado.
11 God's anger is burning on me,
  and God takes me for one of those who oppose the LORD!
12 The whole troop of things God has sent came all together
  and heaped their effects on me, walled me off all around
    where I live:
13 God kept the ones I call brothers and sisters far, far away
    from me,
  and those who know me intimately turned away — that's right! —
    became like strangers to me!
14 Those with my own blood failed me.
  My friends acted as if I was not there!
15 My house guests and those who served me treated me like
    someone unknown —
  I seemed like an odd foreigner in their eyes.
16 I would call to my servant, and he wouldn't answer me —
  I had to beg him to help me.
17 My sickly breath was loathsome to my own wife;
  for the children of my very own body I stunk.
18 Even little boys in the street made fun of me,
  and when I tried to get up taunted me.
19 My closest friends couldn't stand me,
  and the ones I loved turned cold, left me utterly alone.
20 So, here I am, my bones stuck in my flesh to my skin,
  hardly escaped with the skin of my teeth —

21 *Channuni! Channuni! 'Attem re'ai!*

Show me some mercy! show me some mercy! you, my "friends"!
for the hand of God has struck me!

22 Why do you keep on hunting me down, as if you were God?
  Why don't you ever get enough picking away, picking away
    at my life?

23 Oh! if only the matter of my innocence were written down,
          put in a document,
24 chiseled with an iron stylus, cast in lead, fixed deep in rock
     as a lasting witness for when my own words shall not be
               heard later —

25 But no, I know one thing:
     the One who shall defend me and set me free, my *go'el,* lives!
     and that One shall be there later indeed standing up on the dust
          of the earth *as the final One giving witness.*
26 And I, after the worms have shredded my skin,
     be it even out of my flesh,
     I know I shall see God!
27 I shall see God for myself! with my very own eyes!
     and God will not be an opposing stranger to me . . .
     — my very guts are going to pieces inside me —

28 When you say, my "friends," "How shall we hunt him down
     so that the cause of the trouble can be found in him,"
29 fear the sword for yourselves,
     because such hateful, misleading witness is sin worthy of death.
     — Just so you know: there is a judgment coming!

A Congregational Lament
(Versification)

We who are fairly happy people need to have a reservoir of sad song we can use when the hard times come. When a person is broken down by an enemy in God's world — like cancer, evil done by other people, results of bad judgment, imprisonment, divorce, inexplicable illness, an automobile accident, or an untimely death — God's Word of the psalms says, "Sing about it, wounded heart, to the LORD, in the security of the congregated faithful."

   The Genevan melody for Psalm 51 has the quiet, mournful hope to take on our lips when believers as a communion of saints need and want to give voice to their hurt and trust together before God, asking the LORD somehow to come through for God's people at least one more time.

1*

Why, Lord, must evil seem to get its way?
We do confess our sin is deeply shameful;
but now the wicked openly are scornful —
they mock your name and laugh at our dismay.
We know your providential love holds true:
nothing can curse us endlessly with sorrow.
Transform, dear Lord, this damage into good;
show us your glory, hidden by this evil.

2 [Upon someone's imprisonment]

Why, Lord, must he† be sentenced, locked away?
True, he has wronged his neighbor and has failed you.
Yet none of us is innocent and sinless;
only by grace we follow in your way.

---

* Stanza 1 usually is sung first. Then the congregation sings the stanza
  appropriate for the occasion or sings stanza 6.
† Use he/she/they as appropriate.

We plead: repair the brokenness we share.
Chastise no more lest it destroy your creatures.
Hear this lament as intercessory prayer,
and speak your powerful word to make us hopeful.

3 *[For somebody suffering severe illness]*

Why, Lord, must she† be left to waste away?
Do you not see how painfully she suffers?
Could you not change the curse of this disaster?
Amaze us by your mighty sovereignty.
We plead: repair the brokenness we share.
Chastise no more lest it destroy your creatures.
Hear this lament as intercessory prayer,
and speak your powerful word to make us hopeful.

4 *[For anyone undergoing divorce]*

Why, Lord, must broken vows cut like a knife?
How can one wedded body break in pieces?
We all have failed at being pure and faithful;
only by grace we keep our solemn vows.
We plead: repair the brokenness we share.
Chastise no more lest it destroy your creatures.
Hear this lament as intercessory prayer,
and speak your powerful word to make us hopeful.

5 *[Upon untimely death]*

Why, Lord, did you abruptly take him† home?
Could you not wait to summon him before you?
Why must we feel the sting of death's old cruelty?
Come quickly, Lord, do not leave us alone.
We plead: repair the brokenness we share.

Chastise no more lest it destroy your creatures.
Hear this lament as intercessory prayer,
and speak your powerful word to make us hopeful.

6 [Other times of deep hurt]

Why, Lord, must any child of yours be hurt?
Does all our pain and sorrow somehow please you?
You are a God so jealous for our praises —
hear this lament as prayer that fills the earth.
We plead: repair the brokenness we share.
Chastise no more lest it destroy your creatures.
Hear this lament as intercessory prayer,
and speak your powerful word to make us hopeful.

Tune: GENEVAN 51 (Genevan Psalter, 1551 edition)

4 Repentance and Forgiveness

Nothing frees us up like coming clean before God about our sin. Brutally honest prayer to the LORD, admitting guilt and nakedly beseeching forgiveness, brings merciful relief.

Another basic reality, going to the core of our humanity, that God addresses throughout the psalms is our human need to repent of sin and to accept God's gracious forgiveness.

Repentance is so radical for us proud and respectable people that we tend to hedge on our guilt, preferring to work off our guilt-feelings by doing penance or by offering sacrifices. When Luther discovered that "repentance" meant you did not have to do it yourself to make good what was wrong, but only had to "be changed at heart" *(metanoia)* by the Holy Spirit and to accept by faith the Lord's forgiving injunction to "Go, and sin no more!" (Romans 3:21-26; John 8:1-11), then, Luther says, "repentance became a most sweet word to me."

Psalms like 51, 32, 6, 38, and 130, in their cry of repentance, can teach us who have such tricky, self-justifying, flowery ways to elude responsibility for our transgressions how to collapse on our knees with the publican's plea, "Lord, be merciful to me, a sinner!" (Luke 18:9-14). Only then do we come to know the release of *God's forgiveness.* The fundamental experience of being forgiven by God goes beyond understanding. How can I be as clean as a newborn babe in God's eyes when to all appearances I am a dirty, wrinkled person worn out by my sin (John 3:1-21)? Yet, whoever gives up justifying oneself before God can be turned around and is let go scot-free by the Lord, a **new** person (II Corinthians 5:17)!

Saints continue to sin and to stab God in the back. But the Lord's offer of forgiveness, of being a secure hiding place where you can shuck your shame and let go of all the trouble in which you are embroiled, remains in force (Psalm 32:1-7). God's grace is not cheap, since Christ went through hell to overcome the destruction we men and women do to one another and to other creatures in God's world (John 3:16-17). But the psalms proclaim that God's forgiveness is tendered by the Lord to us with the expectation that we pass on this undeserved liberation by forgiving others, even our enemies (Matthew 5:43-48; Proverbs 25:21-22; Romans 12:9-21), lest we show deep down that we are ungrateful for the new start given us by the Lord, and we forfeit its grace (Mark 11:25-26; Matthew 18:21-35). To be truly forgiven entails that we also forgive. So it is a tough-love petition — filled with promise — that Christ taught us to pray in God's ear: "Forgive us our sin, O God, as we have also forgiven those who sinned against us."

Psalm 6

In Psalm 6, the psalmist admits that his life is a mess. He is wasting away in tears. Don't set me straight while you are angry, LORD! prays the psalmist. Restore me gently, because I am fragile.

A tune of David for the choir director, to be played
with stringed instruments and bass

1 LORD God! Please do not set me straight while you are angry!
  Don't try to correct me while you are all wound up!
2 Deal gently with me, LORD, because I am fragile, petering out,
      really —
  Heal me, O LORD, for my very bones are caving in,
3 my deepest self is horribly disturbed —
  and you, LORD, how long will it be before. . . .

4 Please turn around, LORD God, pull my life up out of its mess;
  set me free! simply because of your covenantal mercy,
5 because no one remembers you if they are dead!
  In the grave, who can give you praise?

6 I am utterly worn out from all my groaning:
  I drench my bed every night with my crying,
  where I lie down to sleep is awash with tears.
7 My appearance is wasting away because of the hard times;
  I look old simply because of my constantly being buffeted
        and maligned.

8 Get away from me, all you doers of what's crooked,
  for the LORD God has heard the cry of my weeping!
9 The LORD has heard my plea for help.
  The LORD God has accepted my importunate praying:
10 all my enemies shall be shamed and disoriented;
  those evildoers shall be spun around without warning and
        be brought to shame.

Psalm 32

Psalm 32 was written by David after the desperate throes of Psalm 51 had been mitigated by a time of repentance and painful reflection. Covering up what you did wrong weighs you down with depression: no longer trying to hide your sin from God miraculously has the LORD lift off the burden of guilt. Then God becomes your safe hiding place!

A meditative poem from David's collection

1   That man or woman is a happy one
    whose rebellious misdeed has been forgiven,
    whose offending sin has been covered over.
2   That man or woman is indeed a blessed person
    whose guilty wrong the LORD God simply does not count!
    — I mean, the person in whose spirit
    there is no longer any self-deceit left.

3   When I acted dumb, the very bones of my body felt like splinters
    because of the terrible crying I went through whole days long.
4   Yes, for days and nights your hand weighed down
          on me hurtfully;
    the very pith of my body decomposed as if baked in
          summer heat.
5   Then I opened up and made known to you my sin.
    I did not try to hide my guilty wrong any longer.
    I said, "I will stand up, I will, and confess my rebellious
          misdeeds to the LORD God" —
    but then you! You lifted off and carried away the guilt
          of my awful sinning!

6   For such forgiveness everyone who keeps faith should plead
          to you in the hour of being found out
    — that's right! In the overflowing flooding of untold waters
    such a one would not even get wet!
7   You are my hiding place!

You keep me protectedly safe from the evil that is threatening,
    don't you —
you surround me with the happy shout of certain rescue!

[God's voice]

8 "I will make you perceptive.
   I will give you a vision of the way you are to walk.
   I will give you good counsel, and keep my loving eye upon you.
9 Don't be like the horse, like the mule which has no discernment,
   so that one must curb its strong passion with bit and bridle
   lest it press in upon you."

10 A crooked guilty person has many, many painful troubles:
    but whoever tucks himself or herself in close to the LORD
    God embraces with everlasting, covenanting, gracious mercy.
11 So be happy in the LORD God!
    Laugh and be joyful, you who came through doing what is right!
    Shout jubilantly, everyone who is straight at heart!

Psalm 32 (Versification)

Blessed are the man and woman when forgiven
their willful sin, when God gives them a pardon.
Blessed are the young and old whose guilty wrong
the LORD removes because their hearts come clean.
Your hand brought pain, LORD; day and night I suffered,
so long as I would not confess my evil.
Now that my heart no longer hides its sin,
You lift my guilt away and make me free.

Let every sinful saint who would be rescued
before the flood, repent and plead forgiveness.
We know the wicked harden in their hurts,
but you keep safe those, LORD, who trust in you.
You are our hiding place and certain wisdom!
You will deliver us from stubborn passions.
Let us be joyful as forgiven folk!
Laugh with the LORD: God's grace brings jubilee.

Tune: GENEVAN 32 (Genevan Psalter, 1551 edition)

Psalm 38

Psalm 38 is the prayer of one who is isolated and buckled over with pain, shunned by family, and weak from guiltily realizing that some of the suffering is connected to one's own past sinning. Yet such a troubled person pleads with God to come stand close, right next to me, please. . . .

A song of David, for musical accompaniment as a memorial offering

1 LORD God, do not set me straight while you are angry.
   Please do not discipline me while you are so thoroughly mad!
2 Your destructive blows have gotten to me.
   Your hand has come down heavy on me.
3 There's not a sound spot in my whole body, thanks to
             your cursed punishment:

4 there's no shalom in my bones, because of my sins.
   Yes, my misdeeds have piled up over my head —
   they weigh down on me like a too heavy weight.
5 My bruised-feeling sores, because of my godless stupidity,
             fester and stink!

6 I am buckled over, I'm really messed up.
   Day after day I walk around dejected;
7 that's right, inside my abdomen there's a fevered burning —
   there's not a sound spot in my whole body.
8 I feel numb, utterly beaten,
   yet I want to scream because of the pent-up groaning
             of my heart!

9 My Lord, my deepest desires lie open to you.
   My sighs of longing are not concealed from you.
10 My heart throbs wildly — my strength has petered out,
   even the light in my eyes dims to nothing.

11 My loved ones and close fellows stand over there aloof to me;
   my blood relatives carefully keep their distance.
12 Those who are out to get me set traps for me to walk into;
   those looking out for my ruin promise destruction —
   they stealthily concoct things deceitful, all day long.

13 But I am like a deaf mute who can't hear!
   like a speechless person who can't open the mouth.
14 I'm somebody who just doesn't pick up their hate;
   in my mouth there is no comeback,
15 because I hope for you to come through, Lord God!
   You will hear me, won't you, my Lord, my God?
16 I always said to myself, "Just so those who act big-time
         toward me
   don't get to laugh at my expense when my foot trips me up" —
17 for I am indeed all set to stumble and fall,
   and my painful sorrowing is going to hang around for a
         long time.
18 It's true, I acknowledge my guilty sinfulness.
   I am genuinely concerned about my offending deeds.
19 My living enemies stand strong,
   and those who hate me for no cause grow in number.
20 They pay me back evil for good.
   They bear me a grudge because I strive for what is good! —

21 Do not leave me in the lurch, Lord God!
   My God, do not remain way over there distant from me!
22 Please hurry up to stand next to me,
   O my Lord, my deliverance!

Psalm 51

Psalm 51 has not a single word of excuse, because David was caught by God red-handed in adultery and murder. "I am a pervert!" cries the sinner. "But do not take your Holy Spirit away from me! O God, wash me until I become whiter than snow. Save me from my self! Do not reject my chastened heart yielded up to you as an offering." A later coda incorporates this personal confession of sin into a liturgical worship setting for rebuilding the city of God.

A psalm of David for the music director, composed after the prophet Nathan came to him because David had slept with Bathsheba

1 God! be merciful to me in your covenantal love!
   In your boundless motherly compassion undo my violating act!
2 Scrub me utterly clean of my guilty wickedness!
   Make me pure from my wasteful sin!

3 Yes, I know intimately my dirty deed myself, I do.
   My spoilsome sin is ever in front of my face.
4 I have sinned against you; especially against you have I sinned,
        O God.
   I did evil while you looked on —
   You are perfectly just in your accusation;
   You are utterly right in your judgment.
5 It's true, I was born perverted.
   When my mother conceived me, I was already crooked.
6 I know, you want truth in the gut:
   quietly now teach me that wisdom deep down, O God.

7 Purge me with hyssop that I become pure;
   Wash me until I become whiter than snow.
8 Make me cheerful and happy again.
   Let my very bones you have broken move joyfully once more —
9 Turn your face away, O God, from my wasteful sin.
   Wipe out all my dirty deeds.

10 Create in me a clean heart, O God!
   Give me a steady, fresh spirit inside.
11 Do not expel me from your presence.
   Do not take your Holy Spirit away from me!
12 O God, bring back to me the joyful experience of your
         help again.
   Prop me up — make me a willing obedient spirit.

13 Then I will teach rebels your ways of doing things
   so that sinners will be turned around to come back to you —
14 Deliver me, God, O God of my salvation, undo the
         blood-guilty deeds!
   so that my tongue may jubilate at your trustworthily
         coming through.
15 O, my Lord, let my lips be opened
   so that my mouth may shout out your praise!
16 A sacrifice is not what you want
    — even if I were to give you a burnt offering
   it would not smell sweet to you.
17 My offering, O God, is a chastened spirit.
   O God, a chastened, yielded heart you will not despise, will you?

*[God used later scribes, perhaps around the time of Nehemiah,
to add these closing verses:]*

18 Do good to Zion in your grace, O God.
   Rebuild the walls of Jerusalem.
19 Then you shall take pleasure in offerings of right-doing,
   in offerings that go completely up in smoke, the "total" kind
         of offerings
    — that's the festive time when people will offer whole young
         bulls on your altar!

Psalm 130

Psalm 130 cries out to the LORD from the depths of despair: If you, O God, kept track of guilty wrongdoings, who could ever withstand such judgment! But the LORD God sets people free and wipes out transgressions! Anticipate that merciful, saving Word of the LORD the way a night watchman waits for the light of morning.

A song to sing while walking up to Jerusalem

1 Out of the deepest pits I have always cried out to you, LORD God.
2 Hear my voice now, my Lord.
   Be all ears to the loud sounds of my desperate pleadings!

3 If you were to keep track of guilty wrongdoings,
   O God! my Lord, who could ever withstand such scrutiny?
4 But with you there is Letting-a-man-or-woman-go-free!
   so that you be held in the deepest awe —

5 Yes, I do hope in the LORD God,
   I really anticipate getting the LORD's Word.
6 I watch and wait expectantly for my LORD to come,
   even more than night watchmen keep track of how the
           morning breaks —

7 Israel! You, too, be eagerly open to the LORD God's coming!
   for with the LORD is a Promising-mercy [*chesed*],
   with the LORD are all kinds of being-set-free!
8 Yes, the LORD shall set Israel free
   out of all its guilty wrongdoings. . . .

Psalm 130 (Versification)

Out of the depths I cry, my LORD;
please hear my desperate pleading.
Do not leave me alone, ignored;
provide what I am needing!
If you kept count of guilt and wrong,
my Lord, then who would still be strong?
No soul could stand your scrutiny.

But you forgive those who have erred,
so we may serve you humbly.
I yearn for your redemptive word
to kindle hope within me.
I wait with great expectant sight,
as watchers search for morning light
— come quickly, LORD, to save us!

Hope in the LORD, trust in God's care,
and claim God's promised embrace.
Take heart, you faithful, in despair,
you soon will know the LORD's grace.
The LORD shall rescue Israel
from all its sin — Immanuel!
God's love brings rich redemption.

Tune: AUS TIEFER NOT (Martin Luther, 1524)

5 *Wrestling with the* LORD

When a person has to hang tough for the long haul, direct intimate talk with God can revive the zest of being hopeful and the thirst for the LORD's coming again.

Wrestling in faith with God for rescue and blessing, knuckles bared, fired up with *chutzpah,* is what the LORD wants from God's adopted children (Psalm 91:14-16; Matthew 7:7-11; John 16:23-24). Wrestling with God is not pretty, because it is a matter of life or death. One must not cry "Wolf!" to God if there are no wolves on the horizon. But the LORD does want us to tangle with God to come through. God promises that the prayer of right-doing faithful ones avails much and can change God's mind (Jonah 3; Matthew 15:21-28; Luke 7:1-10; James 5:13-18). Pulling fervently on God in prayer is to pull on a biblical lifeline for our buffeted, Melchizedek ministry in the moil and roil of the world.

It is absorbing and instructive to find that the psalmists mince no words with God. They have a history with God, are familiar with how God does things, and are ready to chew out God for attention: "Listen to us, listen to us crying, LORD!" (Psalm 86:1-7). "We can't go on living with the suffering: You carry it for us, LORD — carry us through the misery, loneliness, uncertainty, and frightening hurt" (Psalm 25:16-21; Psalm 43; Isaiah 63:7-9). "If we have become strangers to You, O LORD, at least show us decent hospitality in this world of yours where we dwell so briefly!" (Psalm 39:12).

Such entreaties in the psalms openly remonstrate with God in an accusing vocative case: "LORD, we belong to you — why leave us in the lurch?" (Psalm 22:1-11; 38:21-22). "How long will you keep on forgetting to take care of us?" (Psalm 13:1-2). "If you let me succumb to this wasting illness, LORD, I can't praise you in the grave, can I?" (Psalm 6:4-5; 30:6-10).

Are the psalms perhaps foreign to our vocabulary because we do not normally find ourselves in dire straits? How can it make sense to pray for our daily manna if the freezer is well stocked with meat? Perhaps our prayers are often just superficial, much too prim and polite in diction for God to give a rough-and-ready answer, because we do not know firsthand the oppressive predicaments the psalmists experienced — left behind as an outcast, covered in feces, facing extinction.

Would to God the psalms could teach us the tensile strength of pleading with the LORD, of wrestling with God, if not for ourselves then as intercessors for others who desperately need protective custody. If we take these psalms on our lips, in our mouth, actually to wrestle earnestly with God, the LORD will indeed give grit to mature our faith and maybe, as the Angel of the LORD did once upon a time for Jacob ("the deceiver"), bless us with a handicap, a thorn in the flesh, to keep God's servants seasoned and humble (Genesis 32; II Corinthians 12:1-10). The well-worn phrase of the prayer Christ taught us has a feisty existential dimension: "Give us today, Lord, our daily manna — the food we need, the emotional well-being, the reflective insight, the wisdom to rule with mercy, O Lord, **lest we perish!**"

Psalm 13

Psalm 13 asks God, How long are you going to forget me? Must I always second-guess whether you hear me with an answer? Keep reassuring me of your enduring love, O LORD.

A psalm of David, for the attention of the choir director

1 How long, LORD God, how long will you keep on forgetting me!
      Forever?
 How long will you hide your face from me?
2 How long must I always be second-guessing such things
      deep inside myself,
 and have worrisome pain in my gut all day long?
 How long will my enemy have me in its triumphant power?

3 Take a good look, O LORD, my God, please hear me with
      an answer!
 Keep my eyes bright with life lest death itself put me to sleep,
4 and my enemies roll in the aisles when they see me about
      to break down —

5 But I still sense I am safe in your covenantal love.
 My deepest heart rejoices in your always coming through
      to the rescue.
6 I will sing out to the LORD!
 Yes, the LORD has always helped me grow more sure of
      God's enduring love.

Psalm 13 (Versification)

How long, O LORD, will you ignore —
how long face me like a closed door?
How long must I brood on what went wrong,
suffer with pain, worry all day long,
blocked by the enemy's cruel war?

Take a close look, LORD, answer prayer!
Keep my eyes bright, safe in your care
lest I succumb to hateful death's hour,
caught in the grip of evil's power
which laughs while I wrestle despair.

But I sense I am safe with you.
Your covenant love remains true.
My heart is happy in your favor;
I celebrate the LORD my savior:
God always has brought me rescue!

Tune: GENEVAN 13 (Genevan Psalter, 1551 edition)

Psalm 25

Psalm 25 confesses that the LORD who is good and kind will see to it that the tricky people are shamed, not those who are meekly walking along the road of justice. Remember how close we used to be, my LORD, confides the psalmist. I'm a little lonely now and am waiting expectantly for you in your faithfulness to come and let me breathe more freely.

Written by David

1 I yield myself up to you, LORD God.
2 With you I feel certain, O God.
   Do not let me be shamed!
   Do not let my enemies maliciously laugh at me!
3 — no, nobody who waits for you will be ashamed;
   those who are tricky for no reason at all, they will be shamed.
4 Get me to know how you act, LORD.
   Teach me how you do things.
5 Bring me along till I follow your kind of faithfulness —
         teach me that!
   for you are my God, the one saving me!
   the whole day I hope, wait to see you coming. . . .

6 Do you remember how close we were, LORD?
   Remember your gracious deeds of promising faithfulness?
   Remember them because they are everlastingly there:
7 Do not remember the sins of when I was growing up!
         my low-down sins
   for **your** good! LORD, remember me with your grace.

8 The LORD God is good and kind:
   That is why God shows those who are confused the right path
         to take;
9 why God lets the meek walk along the road of what is just;
   why God exercises those who are pliable in God's way
         of walking.

10 All the ways of the Lord God are full of grace and trustworthy
    for those who keep intact God's covenanting, obey God's
        commanding Word.
11 For the sake of **your** name! Lord, forgive me my crookedness,
    my proud foolishness — there is so much of it.
12 If you can find a man or woman who fears the Lord God,
    you will meet one whose chosen direction is guided by the Lord.
13 That man or woman rests in joy!
    And their children shall inherit the earth as lords!
14 The Lord God takes those who fear the Lord into
        God's confidence
    and lets them intimately know the bond of God's promises.
15 My eyes remain fastened on the Lord God,
    for God shall extricate my feet out of all traps.

16 Come closer to me, Lord, and be tenderly merciful,
    for I am a little lonely and don't feel so happy-go-lucky.
17 Could you loosen the tightness around my heart,
    and let me breathe more freely?
    Could you get me out of my difficulties?
18 Don't you see my troubles and my weaknesses?
    Take away all the bungled blunders of my sins.

19 Look how many enemies I have, and how desperately, evilly,
        they hate me!
20 O God! Keep me safe! Deliver me from evil!
    Do not let me be shamed, because I put my trust in you!
21 Let innocence and blamelessness before you, Lord, preserve me,
    for I am waiting expectantly for you to come.

Psalm 39

Psalm 39 is a turbulent, daring argument with God for better treatment in our very short lives. You, says the psalmist, are like a clothes-closet moth, LORD, eating away my most prized treasure! Take away your vexing burden and at least give me the godly hospitality in your world that any stranger would deserve!

A melody of David, for the director of music, Jeduthun

1 Once upon a time I said to myself:
   I have got to watch out for my attitude or there will be
               sinning with my tongue.
   I have got to muzzle my mouth as long as the wicked are
               nearby me — or there will be sinning with my tongue.
2 So I stopped my tongue from even moving. I kept still.
   But rather than get better, my vexation grew more agitated.
3 I got all hot inside; I started getting burned up;
   I had to set my tongue loose and talk.

4 So I said: LORD God! LORD God . . . tell me . . . about the
               outcome, the end of the affair of me;
   and tell me how many days I still have so that I may realize
               what a perishable thing I am.
5 Yes, you made the span of my days about as broad as a
               man's hand,
   and my lifetime is like nothing to you —
   a little hot air, that's all a man can make himself out to be,
6 he walks along like a shadow, getting steamed up about nothing,
   he tries to get everything stacked up under control and doesn't
               even know who will take it over after him. . . .

7 At the same time, Lord! now — what did I want?
   Oh, yes, I want . . . my desire! my longing! what I hope for
               and expect! my request . . . that goes out to you, Lord, is:
8 Save me from all my sins!

Do not let me be made the laughingstock of the fools
       around me!
9 — I'll keep quiet. I won't open my mouth. I know, it is you
       who afflicts me —
10 But — but, LORD — take away the vexing burden under which
       you weigh me down,
for I have been wasting away under the pressure of your hand.
11 You discipline a man by punishment for his sins,
and like a clothes-closet moth you eat away his most
       coveted prize —
yes, a little hot air, that's all a man is. . . .
But —

12 Hear my prayer, LORD. Listen to my cry for help!
Do not be unmoved, because I am crying.
Remember, I am a stranger here, a guest, just a sojourner
like all my fathers and mothers before me, your guest, Lord.
13 Don't look at me that way!
Let me become a little more cheerful before I sink away and
       am no more. . . .

Psalm 39 (Versification)

Once I said, "I must keep quiet:
else I sin in harsh dispute.
Just to see the wicked near me
angers me, but I stay mute."
Yet I could not hold my fury,
burned to vent my sharp critique;
then, at last, I had to speak:

"Lord, are you revealing limits,
how my days look in your sight?
Just a breath and fleeting shadow
slipping by in useless flight?
Yes, I know our lives are fragile,
that we seem to work in vain —
all we have is others' gain.

"Why, O Lord, must I be waiting
when my hope is still in you?
Keep me, Lord, from sin and trouble,
from the wrong I would pursue.
Save me from the fool's loud laughter —
I'll be silent, I forgot:
You control my troubled lot.

"But, my Lord, your heavy burden
wears me out and weighs me down.
All your discipline for sinning
hurts and bows me to the ground.
Must you eat away my treasures
like a moth? I'm but a breath.
Are you facing me with death?

"Can't you see, LORD, I am crying?
Do not spurn my sore unrest.
I pass by like those before me,
yet I claim to be your guest!
No more sadness — give me gladness,
be my hope before I cease.
LORD, dear LORD, I beg for peace."

Tune: TYDDYN LLWYN (Evan Morgan, 1800s, Welsh)

Psalms 42 and 43

Psalm 42–43 (probably one psalm, despite the two numbers) has a quietly reassuring refrain which chides the believer who is complaining about God's absence. So you are tearfully thirsting for God the way a parched deer wants fresh water? Skeptics are taunting you about your dejection because God is missing in action? Well, implore the LORD to send you God's light and truth so you may thank and praise God in celebrative worship.

Meditative poetry by the guild of Korah, for the music director

1 As a deer stretches itself out toward the deepest, clearest spot
          of the flowing water,
    that is how I stretch out myself toward you, O God —
2 I am thirsty for God! the living God . . .
    When shall I go in and see God face to face?

3 My tears have become my food day and night,
    because they keep on saying to me all day long,
    "Where and when now is your God going to show up?"

4 So I take to thinking back — I just let myself go inside! —
          about the times
    when I trooped along with the crowd of people to the house
          of God,
    a jumble of happy voices and "Thank you, LORD,"
          "Thank you, LORD!"
    a regular mix-up of dancing celebration! —

5   **Why are you so buckled over deep down, fellow?**
     Why are you getting yourself so worked up?
     Can't you hope in God?
     — Yes, I'll be praising God again sometime, right?
     the One who keeps me safe, my God. . . .

6 I've been all crumpled over on myself inside.

That is why I take to remembering you, O God,
from the Jordan land and the Hermon hills and the
Mizar mountain!

7 Ocean deep roars to ocean deep with the tidal wave voice
of your hurricanes;
all your breakers and storm waves smash over me hard!
8 Day after day I say, "Let the LORD have God's faithful
mercy show!"
And night after night the old song comes to me, a prayer
to the God of my life,
9 I say to God, my Rock, "Why have you forgotten me?
Why must I walk around dejectedly hemmed in because
of the pressuring of the enemy?!"

10 Like a sledgehammer finely smashing my innermost bones
to bits,
the taunting me by my cagey opponents goes on day after day
as they say, "Where and when now is your God going to
show up?"

11 **Why are you buckled over deep down, indeed, fellow!**
Why are you so agitated inside?
Can you not hope in God?
— **Well, sometime, yet, I'll be thanking God again,**
won't I?
the One who saves me, my God. . . .

1 Do me justice, O God!
You argue my case out against the faithless, merciless people
around me!
Help me escape from their deceit and underhandedness,
2 for you are my God! my Stronghold! aren't you?

Why have you shucked me off?
Why must I have a daily life so troubled by the oppressive
maneuverings of the enemy?

3 Send your Light and your Truth so that **they** may lead me!
 Let your Light and your Truth bring me to the mountain
             of your holiness,
 to the places where you reside, [O God]!
4 so that I may step up to the altar of God, the God of my
             jubilant victory all-laughing!
 and thank-praise you with guitar — O God! **my** God!

5   **Why are you buckled over deep down, fellow!**
     Why be so worked up in yourself!
     Put your hope in God!
      — I thank-praise God again, my God!
     the Provident One who always comes through!

Psalms 42 and 43 (Versification)

As a deer craves fresh, clean water,
so do I yearn, God, for you.
I have thirst for living water,
strength your presence can renew.
People threaten me and jeer,
"Your God never will appear!"
All alone I feel mistreated,
weeping constantly, defeated.

Heavy-hearted I remember
times I joined the worship throng
thanking you whose praise engendered
dance and songs which made us strong.
Why must I crumple and hide?
Why be crying deep inside?
Will not God come through as ever?
let me thank my God and savior?

Buckled over far from Jordan,
promised land where we were brought,
I know you still rule Mount Hermon,
why, LORD God, leave me distraught!
Tidal waves break down my guard.
All your storm waves smash me hard.
Yet I daily hopefully moan,
"May your covenant love be shown."

Night and day I walk dejected,
taunted by the enemy,
"Your God has left you rejected — "
Has my Rock forgotten me?
Why must I crumple or hide!
Why be crying deep inside?

Shall not God come through as ever,
let me thank my God and savior. . . .

Vindicate, God, my endeavor
to escape from the deceit
of the crooked-acting clever,
cruelly planning my defeat.
O! my Stronghold! must the wrong
block your love for which I long?
Stop the curses that impede me.
Send your Light and Truth to lead me.

Let your Light and Truth not falter.
O my God, enable me
to be holy near your altar,
jubilant as jubilee.
Why should I crumple and hide!
Why be crying deep inside!
God shall come through now as ever!
I am thanking God my savior!

Tune: GENEVAN 42 (Genevan Psalter, 1551 edition)

Psalm 86

Psalm 86 peremptorily implores the LORD God to bend over and pay attention to my desperate plight, encircled as I am by troublemakers. Only you, my Lord, are God! Gentle, merciful, long-suffering, trustworthy. Surprise everybody now, O God, by doing something wonderful for me. Stop my long-term crying and cheer me up a bit.

An intercessory prayer, probably by David

1   Bend your ear down this way, LORD! Do you hear me?
    For I seem hemmed in all around and miserably don't know
                 where to turn.
2   Take care of me! for I am faithful.
    You are my God! Send your servant some help who trusts in you.
3   O my Lord, be gracious to me —
    I've spent the whole day bawling to you —
4   Could you cheer me up a bit, your servant?
    It's to **you** I extend my heart, Lord!
5   You are good, my Lord, forgiving willingly;
    so rich is your grace to all those blurting out their troubles
                 to you.
6   — Pay attention to my prayer, LORD!
    Bend over and really listen to me, my rather vocal requests:
7   whenever I'm stuck, I cry for you, Lord,
    because I know you will answer me.

8   There is not a one among the gods like you, Lord.
    Nobody does things like you!
9   All the nations of people you made shall come someday
    and fall down before your face, Lord, pay honor to your name,
10 for you are great, doing extraordinarily wonderful things!
    You are God! only you are God —
11 O LORD God, teach me **your** way so that I may walk
               in **your** truth;
    Pull my heart together till it fear only **your** name.

12 O Lord, my God! I want to acknowledge you with my
        whole heart!
   I want to praise your name forever and ever
13 because your covenantal love has been so overwhelming to me:
   You saved me out of the worst dead-ends.

14 O God, malicious, arrogant men are rising up against me!
   a whole crowd of violent troublemakers are out to get me
        and they don't have you in mind at all.
15 But you, my Lord, are a gentle God, merciful, long-suffering,
   full of covenanting love and truth:
16 come here by me; cover me with your grace;
   lend me, your servant, some of your power!
   Help! save me who was your child from very birth!
17 Perform some wonderful thing on me that turns out for good
   so that my enemies may see it and be shamed,
   surprised that you, LORD God! are the one standing by me,
        comforting me. . . .

Psalm 139

Psalm 139 is a most intense expression of intimacy and love about how utterly and unfathomably completely the LORD God knows me, my habits and quirks, even my provisional thoughts, my every day from the womb to the grave. There is nowhere and no time I am not held safe in God's embrace. So let me curse those who hate you, LORD, utters the psalmist. But make certain, O God, that I myself am pure at heart, and hold me with your hand on the way of everlasting life.

A psalm of David written for musical performance

1 You have dug into my life, LORD God, and know me utterly.
2 My sitting down and my standing up — you know that!
   My provisional thoughts you are sensitive to from far away.
3 My just walking around and my lying down you surround
              with your presence.
   Every one of my quirks, I see, you are intimately familiar with:
4 There is not a word on my tongue that you, LORD God,
              do not know exactly.
5 Behind me and ahead of me, you have held me tight.
   You touched me with your hand —
6 it's all too extraordinary, it's beyond me!
   I can't understand such attention!

7 Is there anywhere I could wander where your spirit
              would not be?
   Is there any place I could run away from your being nearby?
8 If I climbed up into the heavens, you would be there;
   If I had to sleep in the grave, there, LORD, you are too!
9 Were I to take the wings of the red early morning sky
   and let myself drift way down to the most remote spot
              of the sea,
10 even there your hand could touch me,
   your right arm would hold me tight.
11 Talking to myself I said, but the Dark, an unhappy gloom,
              might cover me from sight;

the Night, I'm afraid, will swallow me up —

12 But Darkness is not darkness with you,
   and Night is as shining as day,
13 because you created my very insides!
   You delicately braided me together inside the womb
         of my mother —
14 thank you, LORD! that I am so amazingly specially treated!
   whatever you do is most extraordinarily marvelous!

15 You know my self to the core.
   Even though I was conceived in a secluded chamber and artfully
         composed as it were in the lowest bowels,
   my finest bones are not invisible to you.
16 Your eyes saw me when an unformed child!
   Each one of my days being fashioned — not one of them missing!
         — stand written in your book —
17 O God! how unfathomable to me are your doings!
   how overpowering are all of them together!
18 were I to count them up they would number more than
         the grains of sand on the shore.
   — when I am waked from death I will still be with you!

19 O God, would you kill those faithless, godless ones?!
   — get away from me, you unholy, bloody men!
20 those who rebel against you with a smile,
   who use your name for the show?
21 Those who hatefully neglect you, LORD God, shouldn't I
         hate them?
   Those who stand up against you, can I help it if they make
         me stomach-sick?
22 I hate them with a pure hatred.
   They are enemies to me too.

23 O God! Dig into my life and know me heart to heart.
   Test, probe, purify me! and pierce through my thoughts —
24 See whether I be on a road headed for grief,
   And take me by the hand instead on the way of everlasting life.

6 *Comfort*

The comfort God gives for our down times is ongoing and lasts forever.

The *comfort* the psalms give is not what makes you "comfortable." It is the comfort of knowing that you are safe and not alone as you walk through troubled waters. Genuine comfort is not the end of misery or the resolution of problems, but is having somebody you love hold you close while you are hurting.

Because the psalmists as *chasidim* (faithful ones) know both that the living God is their veritable helpmate (Psalm 10:12-14; 30:10; 54:4-5; 72:12-14) and that they personally are each an integral member of a communion, literally surrounded by a host of visible and invisible witnesses to whom they belong (Psalm 42:4; Hebrews 11:1–12:2), they testify to being steadied and comforted as they struggle through sickness, disappointments, obstruction, aging, and the shadows of death. When we listen in on their testimony, we become invited to join their company — not to eavesdrop, but to ease into their tête-à-tête with the LORD and be anointed with the same comfort. Almost by osmosis, as it were, in listening along to the psalmists, one can slip into their comforted fellowship.

The comfort the LORD God bestows on God's faithful, psalm-praying people is mysterious to disbelievers who just want things fixed. God's comfort does not come and go but is ongoing and is often brought by angels unawares — or by ordinary persons from the body of our Lord who by word or by touch promise to stay there with us until the hard time is gone. The psalm voice brings enduring comfort because it recalls what one in distress tends to forget: the world around us **does** embody the merciful LORD's *torah!* The Melchizedek-service of Christ's followers will not abate until the Lord returns in glory! Enemies still sting badly but are essentially defeated! As forgiven sinners, we may plump for God to come through **now**! And without our getting all dressed up!

That is, psalm-comfort brims with promise: the Good Shepherd **is** tending us as a flock (Psalm 23); the Most High God **is** our at-home refuge (Psalm 90:1-2; 91:1-2); God's Son came into the world not to condemn the world but in order to give those who believe in the Messiah everlasting life (John 3:14-21); the LORD God — even if I go under, shouts Job 19:25-27 — **shall establish** the work of our hands for generations still unborn (Psalm 90:17; 115:1-2; I Corinthians 15:50-58). So, be comforted, O sorrowful one, in the embrace of God's powerful, all-encompassing, everlasting presence tendered to you by the attendants of the Holy Spirit, Christ's body here on earth. As Jesus taught all who are God's adopted children to pray, "Our Father in heaven," so God, with fatherly and motherly compassion, holds us dear as Christ's own brothers and sisters, and during our suffering acts to be our consoling mainstay forever and ever and ever.

Psalm 23

Psalm 23 follows up the struggle of Psalm 22 and leads into Psalm 24, where one worships the King of glory in God's holy place. The LORD shepherds you with all God's other sheep, even through the valley of death's shadows, and shall pour your cup brimful with blessings.

A song for musical accompaniment, by David

1 The LORD God is my shepherd too. I lack nothing.
2 In quiet spots of soft green grass the LORD lets me settle down
        in peace.
   My shepherd leads me out to flowing waters giving rest.
3 The LORD brings me back to myself.
   The LORD leads me in the tracks of doing what's right
   for the sake of God's holy Name!

4 Even if I have to walk through the Valley of the shadows
        of Death,
   I will fear no evil
   because you are with me.
   Your shepherd crook and your strong club reassure me.
5 You set table for me with a meal
   right in front of my enemies!
   You anoint my head copiously with oil.
   My drinking cup is overflowing! —

6 It's true! Your covenantal mercy and what's creaturely good
        shall follow me up
   all the days of my life,
   and someday I shall dwell in the house of the LORD God
   for as long as there are days. . . .

Psalm 90

Psalm 90 recognizes that our 70 or 80 years of many troubles and occasional joys flash by like just yesterday to God. But you, my Lord, says the psalmist, have always been the place where we can feel at home. So, gentle us with the smile of laughter, LORD God, by establishing the workings of our dedicated hands.

An intercessory prayer of Moses, a man of God

1 My Lord, you have been our At-home in every generation.
2 Before mountains got born, before earth, this earth was begun,
  from ever and for ever you are GOD!

3 You let men and women turn back to dust;
  You say, "Go ahead back to dirt, you sons and daughters
      of Adam!"
4 I know, a thousand years look like yesterday to you, a day past;
5 You flash flood them away like a brief watch in the night.
  People are a dream, like a plant which sprouts up early
      one morning,
6 breaks ground early on a morning, blossoms full,
  by cool of the evening is withered and dead,
7 so we seem to disappear . . . under your anger? worn out
      by your passionate pace. . . .

8 You have set our guilty, dirtiest deeds in front of you.
  You set our most secret sins right in front of your shining,
      glorious expectant face —
9 Is that why!? all our days get gone, all our years vanish like
      a startled sign
  — because of your terrible, jealous anger!?
10 We get seventy years of days (if we are extra strong,
      maybe eighty),
  but what one boasts of in them is really troublesome labor
      and vanity
  because hip-hop hurriedly it is gone, and we flit along.

11 Who truly understands the solid strength of your anger?!
Who is awestruck at your terribly jealous anger?!
12 Teach us to keep track of our days in such a way that our heart
becomes knowing, wise.

13 Come on back, LORD God! — how long will you wait?
Come on back, and mercifully comfort us, your servants!
14 Like at a new day breaking, fill us so fully of your
gracious faithfulness
that we simply laugh out loud, merrily enjoy ourselves the rest
of our life!
15 Make us laugh for just as many days as you made us cry,
humiliated.
Make us happy, Lord, for just as many years as you had us
suffer evil.
16 Show us, your servants, your wonderful acts again!
and let our children see your glorious power!

17 May the gentle laugh of the Lord, our God, rest upon us,
And the workings of our hands,
You will bring that further for us, will you not?
Yes, the work of our hands, establish it solidly, [Lord]!

Psalm 91

Psalm 91 declares that the LORD God is our place-to-stand even in the dark night of tribulation. Under the cover of God's wings and with the protection of God's angels you cannot be destroyed, but shall eventually conquer even the Dragon! God's voice personally ends the psalm: "Because you know my Name, I shall deliver you from living in fear and give you peace."

1 Whoever feels at home in the presence of the Most Glorious God
   shall be able to pass the night
   in the shadow of the Almighty One,
2 for that person can say to the LORD God,
   "My sanctuary! My Place-to-stand! My God in whom I
            am trusting!"

3 The LORD God shall extricate you from the trap of the Hunter!
   God will save you from the sting of Death!
4 The LORD shall cover you with God's wings;
   under God's wings you can run to hide.
5 Do not be afraid of midnight terror
   or of sickness that stalks people in the daytime
6 or of pain that creeps up on one in the twilight
   or of crippling disease that strikes while the sun shines:
7 a thousand may collapse right next to you,
   ten thousand may be struck down; but you shall not perish —
   God's truth shall protect you, fence you in,
8 while letting you see with your own eyes
   how the godless are paid in full.

9 You have said, "The LORD God **is** my sanctuary!"
   You have taken the Most Glorious God as your At-home!
10 Therefore Destruction cannot get you;
   disaster shall never enter the door where you are living:
11 for God Almighty has made you a charge of God's angels,
   ordering them to guard you in all that you do.

12 They shall hold you up by their hands
   so that you do not even stub your foot against a stone,
13 so that you can walk past roaring lions and poisonous snakes,
   so that you can step on and crush the lion and even . . .
             the Dragon!

[Then God's voice itself ends the psalm]

14 "Because he or she has held fast to me, I shall save them!
   Because she or he knows my name, I shall deliver them!
15 I will hear each one when that person cries out to me;
   I will be with them in the terribly dark days,
   free them from the Darkness, and bring them glory!
16 I will let him and her live peacefully on and on,
   because I shall let them see my salvation!"

John 3

John 3 brings good news to intellectuals like Nicodemus, who prefer to debate what is and is not "possible" rather than admit they too are looking for comfort in their life. Jesus comforts everybody by revealing that he came not to condemn the world but to bring redemption from evil, simply because God loves the whole world God created — mountains, trees, animals, as well as humans. Come out of the dark, says the Lord, by faith, you men, women, and children, into the comforting light of everlasting life.

Jesus is speaking to the intellectual leader Nicodemus at night:

14-15   "Just as Moses once lifted up the *bronze* serpent in the desert, so must the Son of man be lifted up, so that everyone who comes believing may have in him everlasting life.

16-18   "Yes, God really loved the whole world so much that God gave the only begotten Son God had, so that everyone who comes to be believing in him should not be destroyed, but has everlasting life! God, you know, did not send the Son into the world to condemn the world, but in order that the world might be saved through the Son. Whoever is believing in the Son is not condemned. Whoever is not believing in the Son has already been judged, because he or she has not believed in the name of the only begotten Son of God.

19-21   "And this is the judgment: The light has come into the world, but people loved the darkness rather than the light because their deeds were evil. Everyone who is determined regularly to do what is wickedly mean hates the light and does not come into the light for fear that their deeds be exposed. Whoever is doing the truth, however, comes to the light, that his or her deeds may be clearly seen to have been fashioned in *the will of* God. . . ."

7 Trusting God

Trusting the LORD to carry us through difficulties leads to our being surprised by receiving more than we need, so we want to dance at the surplus of God's grace.

Trusting God is not so much a concept the psalms exposit as it is the very lifeblood of their biblical message: the LORD is the trusted liege to whom we privileged human vassals are bound in fealty. It is not an onerous burden (Matthew 11:25-30) to address God on bended knee as *Adonai* ("my Lord"). It is the basic, normal way to accept our given status as servants, stewards, ministers (*'abadim*) in the LORD's city and vineyard (Matthew 20:1-16; 21:28-41; I Corinthians 3:5-9).

Just as the LORD's comfort attends suffering without necessarily ending the distress, so the fundamental *chesed* (enduring covenantal mercy) of the LORD which anchors our trust in God is sure, but does not necessarily deliver what is wanted "on demand." God is trustworthy in the way a good ripe melon is trustworthy: a good melon gives a little to the pressure of one's testing hand, yet holds firm. Trusting God, expecting sustenance or protection, pushes on the LORD for a response, utterly sure of God's merciful firmness, even if there be a delay in God's servicing the need. The psalmist is certain that a night of weeping will be followed in the morning by broken cries of joy (Psalm 30:15). God keeps all our tears in a bottle to document our everlasting life (Psalm 56:8)! The LORD shall without a doubt reinstate the meek who have been humiliated (I Samuel 2:8; Psalm 116:5-7; Matthew 5:3-12).

The psalms embody this incredible childlike trust in the LORD because the psalmists are convicted of God's *chesed* (Exodus 34:6-7) and accept the truth that God's timing and wisdom are beyond our human calculation (Psalm 90:3-7; Ecclesiastes 3:10-11; I Corinthians 1:18-25). Christ's quoting Psalm 22 on the cross testifies that trusting God does not discourage but underlies wrestling with God: Christ berates God for turning away God's face (Psalm 22:1-11) and letting him be prey to enemies (Psalm 22:12-21); yet Christ knew the last paragraph of the psalm too (Psalm 22:22-29) and was counting on the LORD God's coming through with restoration, resurrection, and peace, because the merciful LORD always finally gives you more than you expect.

As you live into the psalms and come to breathe the reality of being embraced by the LORD's *torah* and the enabling grace of God which outfits us with the order of Melchizedek for doing God's will in the world, you realize that nothing creatural is trivial to the LORD. Our perils (Jonah 2), arthritis (Psalm 92:10), the taste of a peach (Ecclesiastes 3:12-13), the hairs of our head (Matthew 10:28-33), not to speak of our deaths not mentioned in newspaper obituaries (Psalm 72:12-14), are all precious to the LORD. Because the allegiance between vassal and lord is mutual — although God is faithful even when we break faith (II Timothy 2:8-13) — this heartbeat of the psalms — trusting the LORD — begins after a while to sound with the pulse of any listeners. Then our petitions for matters great or small take on the quality of utter trust, because we are assured that the Holy Spirit will intercede for our deepest desires far beyond what we humans are able to do, making our requests acceptable to the LORD (Romans 8:26-27). Then our trusting prayers will rhyme with the fervent doxological acclaim: "**Yours** is the kingdom, the power, and the glory forever."

Psalm 30

Psalm 30 asks God's faithful folk to celebrate the truth that after the brief night of weeping will certainly come the morning with its broken cries of joy. Faced with death I bawled to you, LORD, to become my helpmate, and you have indeed turned my sadness into dancing!

A David song written for a consecration service of the house of God

1 I am celebrating you, LORD God, because you pulled me back up;
   you did not let my enemies enjoy themselves at my expense.
2 LORD, my God, I cried out to you, and you have made me
         whole again —
3 LORD, you have raised me up and away from the grave!
   You have let me breathe again! after being so close to those
         who have gone down into the opened earth.

4 O you faithful folk of God — all of you — sing out and
         play music to the covenantal LORD God!
   Let there be thanksgiving in remembering God's holy presence:
5 if sudden ill wrinkles for a little while from God's
         grievous anger,
   our having life and being alive issues from the LORD's
         gracious favor.
   If some evening you have to spend a night weeping,
   there shall be — count on it! — broken cries of joy when
         it is morning.

6 I said to myself, I did, when I was disarmed, at ease,
   "I shall never be shaken up."
7 LORD God, by your gracious good will you had set me up sturdy,
         a mountain of solidified strength;
   but when you turned your face aside, I was shaken,
         completely bewildered.
8 I called out to you, LORD God! — I begged my LORD for mercy —

9 "What good is my blood to you? in my going down into the
  bottomless pit?
  Can dust praise you? Can broken clods of earth announce
  your steadfast faithfulness?
10 Hear me, O LORD God, be gracious to me!
  O LORD God, be my helpmate. . . ."

11 Tja! You have turned my weeping about death, you have
  turned it around for me, LORD, into dancing!
  You have undone my sackcloth of mourning, and girded me
  with gladness!
12 so that my deepest insides may sing and play music for you,
  and I not be devastatedly stilled —
  O LORD God, my God, I will give you thanks forever and
  ever and ever!

Psalm 56

Psalm 56 reveals that God keeps all our tears in a bottle because our suffering from wicked bullies who harass God's people troubles the LORD greatly. God keeps track of our buffeted daily agenda, hears the complaints of wounded believers, and shall indeed stand up and make living genuinely secure for those who trust the LORD.

Song text by David for the cantor to the tune of "The silenced dove far, far away," written after the episode when the Philistines had him trapped in Gath (see I Samuel 21:10–22:1)

1 Be merciful to me, O God!
   because people are chafing at the bit to hurt me,
   all day long they press in viciously to mishandle me.
2 My enemies stalk me all day long,
   yes, many of them high-handedly bully me!

3 On the day when I can't help but become afraid,
   I still do somehow feel safe with you.
4 Near God I can still find cheer in what God is saying.
   With God I feel myself secure; I don't need to be afraid:
   what can mortal flesh do to me!

5 But my antagonists give a nasty twist all the time to whatever
            I say;
   everything that comes to their mind they slant it to be bad
            for me.
6 They provoke things, they lie in wait to ambush me;
   they dog my footsteps like ones who are trying to end my life:
7 for such wicked harassment get rid of them, LORD!
   O God, in anger cut those people down to size!

8 I know, you have kept track of my travail.
   You personally collect all my tears in your wineskin bottle
   — that's true, right!? they are all inscribed in your account book
            of Life!

9 So my enemies will be spun around backwards
  on the day I cry out to you —
  I know that with experiential certainty:
  Yes, God does stand up for me!
10 With God, whose speaking I cherish,
  with the LORD God whose word I revere:
11 with God I feel myself secure, trustworthily cared for, I don't need
          to be afraid:
  what could anybody human really do to me?!

12 The vows vowed to you, O God, weigh on me:
  I should like to make good on songs of thanksgiving for you,
13 for you have rescued my life from a dead end!
  That's right! You saved my feet from stumbling around in circles
          so that I could walk to and fro, dance!
  before the face of God in the light of genuine living!

Psalm 56 (Versification)

[Spoken softly] Be merciful to me, O God!

1

There's people out to hurt me bad.
They menace, play the bully.
When I can't help but be afraid,
O God! protect me fully!

2

They dog my steps, provoke my life,
and twist my words to lies.
O LORD! expose their evil plans
and cut them down to size!

[Congregational line of song] Be merciful to me, O God!

3

I know, my LORD, you keep good track
of all the pain and trouble,
collect my tears like broken jewels
and save them in a bottle.

[Repeat this stanza quietly]

[Then congregational line of song] Be merciful to me, O God!

4

The enemies shall be undone
the day God hears my plea.
I know with utter certainty
God does stand up for me!

5

What mortals can destroy my life!?
The LORD God's Word is sure.
I do not need to be afraid:
God's arms hold me secure.

[Spoken] Thank you for your mercy, LORD!

6

It's time to offer thanks to you,
to dance before your face.
O God, you rescued me from death
to live a life of grace!

[Solo/congregation sing] Thank you for your mercy, LORD! Amen!

Tune: GIOIA IN GOD'S BOTTLE BLUES (Calvin Seerveld, 2001)

Psalm 62

Psalm 62 teaches that only God is the Rock to which one can run for refuge. Aggressive deception, accumulation of goods, importance gained by violence all bring agitated insecurity. Only near God can a person find the stillness of peace.

A David psalm for the choir director in the Jeduthun style

1 Only near God do I myself quiet down.
  Yes, from God comes my salvation.
2 God alone is my rock and my salvation, my stronghold
   — I shall not be shaken up!

3 Oh, how long will you batter a person,
  all of you — ready to murder!
  shrieking as if at the collapse of a wall,
  at the crumbling of a stone fence.

4 They scheme on how to knock a person down from his position
       of authority.
  They enjoy being deceptive.
  They praise you with their mouth, but deep inside they
       are cursing.

5 Only near God do I myself find quietness,
  for only from God does sure hope come to me.
6 God alone is my rock and my salvation, my stronghold
   — I shall not be shaken.
7 With God is my freedom and my glory,
  My mighty Rock! — God is my place to run for safety.

8 Trust in God at all times, O people.
  Pour out your heart before God —
  God is the place for us to run for safety!

9 Ordinary humans are but a breath of hot air;
   Important people are a mirage —
   put in a weighing scale they would all go up,
   altogether nothing more than a little hot air.

10 Do not trust in oppressive violence.
   Never count on anything stolen.
   If your resources grow,
   still do not set your heart on them.

11 One thing God has said,
   Yes, two things I have heard God say:
   (1) Mighty power belongs to God, and
   (2) Merciful covenantal love comes from you, my Lord.
12 Yes, you — you requite every child, woman, and man
   according to what they actually do.

Psalm 62 (Versification)

Near God alone do I find peace.
God brings me rescue and release
from all the evils that could shake me.
Enemies strike me like a wall;
they hatefully would make me fall,
but God my Rock keeps me in safety.

Only with God can I find hope.
God sets me free and gives me scope
to withstand those who tempt to do wrong.
Antagonists entrap my feet,
connive, confuse with bold deceit;
but God is my protective stronghold.

Trust God completely at all times.
Pretentious mortals are but signs
of temporary puffs of hot air.
Violent predators soon die;
riches can never satisfy.
Spill God your heart, and do not despair.

Almighty power rests in God's hand.
Your covenantal love has planned,
my Lord, to keep us in your embrace.
That you requite our deeds is clear;
thank you, the meek may cast out fear:
your strength and mercy is our safe place.

Tune: GENEVAN 62 (Genevan Psalter, 1551 edition)

Psalm 92

Psalm 92 thanks the LORD by making melody for the wild-ox strength God has given persons of integrity. Those who do what is right see through the accomplishment of the wicked — their successes will be demolished. The just who live by faith remain succulent and shall bear fruit even in old age.

A psalm to be sung, a song for the Sabbath Day

1 Good it is to thank the LORD God out loud!
   to play around tunefully in your Name, O Most High!

2 to proclaim your covenantal love at every sunrise
   and thankfully witness to your steadfast faithfulness
           through every night,

3 to make music on the ten-stringed lute and on the harp,
   with nimble-fingered intermezzi played on the lyre,

4 for you have made me joyful, O LORD God, with your
           great deeds —
   I rejoice at the works of your hands!

5 How great are your works, O LORD God!
   How unfathomably deep are your thoughtful plans!

6 A stupid person will never get it,
   a fool will never understand that

7 while the wicked may flourish like lush green grass
   and all the accomplishments of deceptive forces seem brilliant,
   it happens in the context of their total destruction.

8 But you, O LORD God, are to be exalted forever and ever!

9 That's indeed right — your enemies, O LORD God,
   yes, that is certainly right — your enemies will be demolished!
   All the impressive deeds of uncanny deception shall be scattered
           to the winds —

10 However,
    you increase my strength to be like that of a wild ox,
    you anoint me with refreshing ceremonial oil.

11 My eyes see clearly those who stalk my steps;
   my ears hear acutely how those who rise up against me —
           their success in deceit — how they are broken to bits.

12 The person with integrity flourishes like a palm tree,
   grows mature like a cedar on Mount Lebanon.
13 Planted in the house of the LORD God
   those doing what is just keep on sprouting buds in the
           courtyards of our God.
14 Those who do what is right keep on bearing fruit even
           when they grow old —
   they remain fresh and juicy — succulent in old age,
15 able to reveal how thoroughly right-doing is the LORD God,
   my Rock, in whom there is no crookedness.

Psalm 92 (Two Versifications)

Sing praise to God, be playful, God's covenant love is sure:
sunrise and night endure to gladden, make us grateful.
My happiness, O LORD, needs skillful music and voice
to help me laugh, rejoice, and celebrate your great deeds.

Why wicked seem to flourish can not be understood
until their brilliant good is seen to slip and perish.
Fools stupidly avoid your glory, practice deceit,
but you plan their defeat — God's enemies are destroyed.

LORD God, how strong you made me, stout as a strong wild ox!
Your hand anoints my walk with healing oil of safety.
Now those who stalked my steps, placed traps to ambush, trick me,
I clearly hear and see, shall, yes, themselves be laid waste.

Just persons thrive like palm trees, like cedars which mature;
planted near God, secure they always blossom with ease.
Those who do right stay fruitful even when they grow old.
Their aged fertile hold shows God, my Rock, is truthful.

Tune: GENEVAN 92 (Genevan Psalter, 1562 edition)

The LORD enjoys a hot guitar, with drums and sax to cook it.
The LORD enjoys a hot guitar, with drums and sax to cook it.
God moves sometimes it seems so slow,
but my LORD the Rock ain't crooked.

I watch the wicked get ahead; they know the ropes so well.
I watch the wicked get ahead; they know the ropes so well.
"Yeah, those poor enemies," says God,
"they're finding the road to hell!"

I'm getting old, bones drying up, not growing like a tree.
I'm getting old, bones drying up, not growing like a tree.
"Oh, don't you worry," says the Lord,
"You'll get good fresh sap from me!"

The Lord enjoys a hot guitar, with drums and sax to cook it.
The Lord enjoys a hot guitar, with drums and sax to cook it.
God moves sometimes it seems so slow,
but my Lord the Rock ain't crooked.

Tune: BLUES 92 (Calvin Seerveld, 1999)

Psalm 116

Psalm 116 utters plainly the crux of real trust: "I love the LORD because God hears me when I cry and pray." God spills over with compassion! God kept me from killing myself by my walking into ruin! Oh, yes! I'll toast the LORD with the communion cup of victory: "Cheers for Yahweh!"

1 I love the LORD because God hears me when I cry and pray.
2 Yes, God bent God's ear down to me, and I'll talk about it the rest
      of my life!
3 I was caught in a dead end.
The cramp of the grave had a hold on me;
pain and trouble kept hurting.
4 So I called out loud on the name of the LORD:
LORD God, please! get me out — save my life!

5 Full of mercy is the LORD God, just — yes — but our God
      spills **compassion** over!
6 The LORD God takes loving care of those open to temptation —
when I was cut down to size, God took care of me —
7 So calm down, fellow; the LORD has given you what was good!

8 That's so.
You got me out of the dead end.
You have stopped my eyes from filling with tears!
You have kept me from walking into ruin —
9 Yes!
I may walk around in front of God's nose on the earth
      where people are alive!
10 Even when I said, "How utterly miserable I am,"
      I kept faith, LORD.
11 Worked up and distraught, when I said, "You can't trust anybody
      — they lie," *I did still hold on believing you,* LORD.

12 What shall I give the LORD God?
so many lovely surprises God has given me.

13 I know, I shall toast the Lord with the cup of victory —
Cheers for Yahweh!
14 I will do what I vowed the Lord God I would too, and I'll do it
right among God's people.

15 The death of one of the Lord's simple believers costs God a lot;
16 And I am one of your serving believers, isn't that so, Lord?
I am your serving believer, just a servant —
is that why you got me out of what hurt!

17 Yes, I will really offer thanksgiving to you:
Cheers for Yahweh!
18 I mean it, I will do what I vowed to God, and I'll do it among
the faithful,
near the house of the Lord God, right in the middle
of Jerusalem —

Glory, Hallelujah!

Jonah 2

Jonah 2 is the fugitive prophet's prayer of thanksgiving after the LORD God saved him from a watery grave in the turbulence of the sea. Even in the scary throes of death I tried to reach you, O Holy One! Now that you have kept me alive, I want to offer up to you everything I vowed: to be a *living* sacrifice in your merciful service.

2 Squelched to the extreme, I still kept calling out to the
        LORD God,
  and God answered me!
  Deep down, as it were, in the bowels of the grave, I bawled out
        for help,
  and you heard my voice!

3 Something like a whirlpool sucked me down to the bottomest
        vortex of the waters,
  and the swirling mass closed in on me.
  All your breakers and your smashing waves rolled me over
        and over,
4 and I thought to myself, It is finished with me,
  tossed completely away from where your eye reaches —
  Oh! if I could only get a look at the place of your Holiness!

5 The water choked me down till I couldn't breathe.
  The deepest depths of the sea closed in and on and over me.
  Seaweed tied my head in tangles.
6 I sank. I sank down to the deepest sucking points of the
        mountainous waves —
  The earthland! vistas of the earthland closed off from me
        forever!
  But out of that destructive pit you snatched me up and
        away alive!
  O YAHWEH, my God!

7 When my very life breath inside me was being snuffed out,
   I still remembered the LORD God.
     My prayer still kept going out to you, trying to reach the place
       of your Holiness.
8 Those who hold on to the empty hot air of no-gods have to
       abandon their holdfasts;
9 but I, with the happy sound of thankful song, I want
       to sacrificially offer up to you
   everything I vowed I would make good on and bring
       to completion —
   triumphant deliverance is only with the LORD God YAHWEH!

Jonah's Song (Versification)

In the fish for three days buried,
I kept calling, "Save me, LORD!
Keep me from the hellish graveyard,
lost at sea, by you ignored."
Tossed and turned beneath rough waters,
choking in your whirlpool sea,
I cried out, "My life is finished!"
but, O LORD, you answered me.

Down to death the waves had pulled me,
down, entombed where none survive.
Seaweed round my head was tangled;
water swallowed me alive.
"Is God's face now gone forever?
Have I forfeited God's care?"
No! You saved me from destruction,
raised me, LORD, and heard my prayer.

In despair, afraid of dying,
I implored you anxiously.
Unlike those who shirk their promise,
I bring offerings thankfully.
Take my life I vowed to give you;
bless my joy, and make it known.
Let all know that sure deliverance
comes from God the LORD alone.

In the tomb for three days buried,
Christ had gone to face the worst.
Just as God took care of Jonah,
God raised Jesus as the first.
All who know the Holy Spirit
shall defeat the grip of sin.

Christ has conquered death and Satan,
let the jubilee begin!

Tune: EIFIONYDD (John Ambrose Lloyd, 1800s, Welsh)

8 God-promises

The LORD God's promises of deliverance from evil and the Rule of shalom acoming are freely offered to all who hear the Word to be daily obedient like God's servant the sun.

God-promises in the psalms are not mere talk and are not parochial. They are efficacious and offered to anyone who hears the voice of the LORD, because God is good, says Psalm 100:5. Jesus emphasized that only God is good (Mark 10:18). Only God-promises are worth their weight in outcome.

God-promises are a multi-splendored array of the LORD God's central covenant to lead all proper creatural endeavors to their fulfillment. Sunrise and sunset (Psalm 19:1-6; Judges 5:31), seedtime and harvest (Genesis 8:20-22), animals begetting healthy animals (Psalm 104:24-30) — through them all, God-promises are being kept. When bread and wine satisfy human hunger (Psalm 34:10; 81:16), and children can play safely in the streets (Zechariah 8:1-8), and grandparents watch their grandchildren profess their faith in the LORD (Psalm 128:5-6) — then God-promises are being consummated. And when the brokenhearted are given a new start (Psalm 34:18), and the buckled-over turn their disconsolate refrain into one of hopeful confidence (Psalm 42:5, 11; 43:5), and the Messiah actually comes historically out of the stump of Jesse, preaching freedom from captivities like prisons and addictions — all of this an earnest on the Judgment Day when evil shall be permanently ended and an incredible cornucopia of shalom be enjoyed (Isaiah 61:1-7; Luke 4:16-22; 7:18-23; Isaiah 11:1-10) — then God-promises are indeed making waves!

God-promises scatter blessings indiscriminately if people come to hear them in faith and lay claim to God's offer, as the Ninevites did in Jonah's day (Jonah 3), as the eunuchs in Israel did after the Babylonian exile (Isaiah 56:1-6), and like the oddball judges mentioned in Hebrews 11:32-34. God even does not desire the destruction of evildoers, but holds out the promise of their turning around in their tracks (Ezekiel 18:21-32).

A special reach of God-promises comes when believers pray for them to be opened up to those who may be ignorant, indifferent, or antagonistic to the LORD, or be applied to a remnant of believers at bay. Intercessory prayer is Melchizedek-service par excellence, because God-promises are then activated by a community, a communion of saints, so God is not privatized. The God-promise to have fellow believers correct our walk with the LORD and to pray us away from defaming God and neglecting our neighbors in need (Psalm 141:5; Matthew 25:31-46) is a rich tribute to the LORD's patience with us men and women and to God's willingness never to test us beyond what we can endure (I Corinthians 10:1-

13). Jesus reiterated this deep God-promise when he taught his disciples to pray, "O Lord, lead us not into temptations that are subtle devilish traps." And God's promisory voice responds: "Because you know my Name, I shall free you from Darkness and show you my salvation" (Psalm 90:14-16).

I Samuel 2

I Samuel 2 sings out Hannah's jubilant, intercessory magnificat, since the LORD vindicated her shamed trust by giving her the birth of a child, Samuel ("God heard"). It is the LORD who knocks the proud prostrate and raises up the weak who have been ground down into the dust. It is the LORD who sends death and gives life! Praised be the LORD God who lifts up the head of God's anointed ones!

1 My heart is jubilant in the LORD God!
   God has lifted my head up again!
   I dare open my mouth now before my enemies,
   because I am so happy in your Grace, LORD.
2 Nobody is holy like the LORD God!
   There is no one next to you.
   There is simply not a protection like our God.

3 Don't talk so much! such high-blown words;
   don't be so cheeky and disparaging, my enemies!
   For the LORD God is a knowing God —
   it is the deeds God takes careful note of.

4 Mighty men are filled with fear,
   while people starting to stumble pull themselves together
        with some hidden strength.
5 Those stuffed with food have to hire themselves out to get bread,
   while those who were hungry are able to celebrate restfully.
   The barren woman bears half-a-dozen children!
   while she with many — her spring dries up.

6 The LORD God sends death and gives life!
   The LORD God lets people go to hell and raises them up and out
        of their graves.
7 The LORD God makes people poor and makes people rich.
   The LORD God knocks people down to the ground, yes,
        and raises them up high.

8 The LORD God picks up out of the dust the weak who
        have fallen.
    God pulls those who have been pushed around out of
        the manure pile,
    and sets them next to princelings, and gives them a
        glorious throne of their own.
    The very pillars of the earth on which God has fixed
        the inhabited continents belong to the LORD.

9 The LORD takes good care of the way God's saints walk.
    But those who would do without the LORD, God will demolish
        in the Dark
    because no man or woman succeeds at anything by their
        own strength.
10 Those who keep fighting against the LORD God will get broken;
    the Highest holy One in the heavens shall break them in pieces.
    The LORD God rules every bit of the earth!
    God gives strength to God's ruler!
    and lifts up the head of God's anointed one!

Hannah's Song (Versification)

My heart is filled with joy, my body thanks God.
Praised be the LORD who took away my shame.
Proud enemies shall never more torment me.
God knows and judges cruel talk and deeds.
You only, LORD, remain a Rock of safety.
No one is holy like God our LORD.

God breaks down armed might, gives the feeble fresh strength.
God thwarts the greedy, finds the hungry food.
Those with abundant children God can undo,
but grants the barren fruitfulness renewed.
The LORD brings death, and authors every child's birth.
God made the grave: God resurrects to life.

God's touch brings poverty as well as true wealth,
humbles the haughty and exalts the meek.
God brings the helpless into ruling power;
God saves the outcast from obscurity.
Since God the LORD created this entire world,
life's earthly order rests on God the Rock.

The LORD picks carefully the way God's saints walk.
God leaves the godless standing in the dark.
None shall succeed in history by brute force.
Those who keep fighting God's Word shall be lost.
The ruling LORD prepares reward for past deeds:
glory for those anointed in Christ's Name!

Tune: GENEVAN 37 (Genevan Psalter, 1551 edition)

Psalm 34

In the Hebrew text, Psalm 34 is an alphabetic acrostic, in which every other verse begins with the successive letter of the alphabet. The psalm cites how the Angel of the LORD protects whoever stands in awe of God and works at peace-making. The LORD God holds tenderly those whose heart is broken and gives a new start to those whose spirit has been crushed.

A song written by David after the time when he feigned madness in front of [Achish]-Abimelech so that the Philistine overlord got rid of him and David went safely on his way (see I Samuel 21:10-15)

At all times I will praise the LORD; my God's praise is constantly
    in my mouth!
Be glad when you hear this, you who are doing poorly: all of me
    exults in the LORD!
Come, magnify the LORD with me! Let us all together exalt the
    Name of the LORD!

Delivered from everything I dreaded! That's the way the LORD
    has responded whenever I pleaded with God for help.
Embarrassed and shamefaced — never! Your look will be radiant
    if you look up to the LORD.
Forlorn — this is one fellow who cried out desperately, and the LORD
    heard and saved him from all of his dead ends.

Get this: the Angel of the LORD! protectively surrounds those who
    stand in awe of the LORD and hauls them out of troubles.
Happy will the strong person be who runs to take refuge with the
    LORD: taste it, see for yourself how good the LORD God is!
Indeed, you saints, wait expectantly upon the LORD God since those
    who quietly wait upon the LORD shall lack nothing!
Just the opposite from young lions who lack what they need and
    go hungry: those who keep asking the LORD will never
    fail to receive what is thoroughly good.

Listen to me, come on, you fellows, I will teach you to stand in awe
     of the LORD God.
Man or woman — who does not desire a lifetime, is not deeply
     driven to wish for days full of experience that are
     really good?
Never let your tongue slip into trivializing talk or your lips
     twist words misleadingly.
O yes, shun evil and do what is good; seek shalom — pursue
     the fullness of peace!

Present with those who do what is just are the watchful eyes
     of the LORD, God's ears attend to their cries.
Remembrance of those who do what is unjust: the face of the
     LORD God is turned to wipe it off from the face of the earth!
Screams of the just *who are violated,* however, the LORD God
     does hear, and shall surely snatch them away from their
     terrible distress —
The LORD God is near to those whose heart has been broken
     and gives a new start to those whose spirit was crushed.

Untold evil sufferings do afflict whoever does what is right,
     but the LORD God shall indeed snatch that man or woman
     out of it all.
Verily, God looks out for all of your bones — not one of them
     shall be broken!
Wicked folk shall be killed by godless evil, and those who hate
     the one who does what is right shall undergo punishment.
Yes, the LORD God sets free the life of those who serve God:
     everyone who takes refuge with the LORD shall not
     undergo God's condemnation.

Psalm 81

Psalm 81 recalls God's people feasting at their deliverance from Egyptian slavery. Then the LORD updates God's old promises: I will satisfy you with plenty if you will heed my jealous love; otherwise, your stubborn hearts will be your downfall.

By Asaph, for musical performance on gittith strings

1 Cheer God who is our strength!
  Make a lot of noise for the God of Jacob!
2 Pick up the stringed instruments, and start playing
          the tambourines!
  the melodious zither along with the harp —
3 Blast the trumpet at new moon, at full moon again!
          for the day of celebration!
4 The Passover, you know, is regulation for Israel,
  an injunction declared by the God of Jacob.
5 God established the Passover memorial ordinance at the time
          of Joseph,
  when God self walked out one night over the land of Egypt.

  I am hearing words I hardly recognize. . . .

[The LORD speaks:]

6 I took the weight off their shoulders;
  their fists broke free from the laden baskets.
7 You cried aloud in your dead end, and I lifted you out!
  Veiled in a thundering cloud I made you an answer.
  At the waters of Meribah I put you to the test. . . .

8 Listen, my people, I have to protect you! —
  If you would only hear, Israel, what I have to say —
9 Let there be no strange god among you!
  Do not be asking favors from some foreign god!

10 I, the LORD God YAHWEH, am **your** God,
    the One who brought you up out of the land of Egypt:
    open your mouth wide and I shall fill it full.

11 But my people did not listen to my voice.
    Israel did not go along with me.
12 So I left them, let them in the blocked stubbornness
        of their hearts go;
    they went their way in their own clever thought-patterns. . . .

13 Would that my people would listen to me!
    Would that Israel walked in my ways . . .
14 how quick I would smash their enemies!
    how quick my hand would push back those who crowd them;
15 those scorning the LORD God would cringe before my folk —
    and my people's time would be for keeps, everlasting. . . .
16 The LORD would feed them from the best grain!
    Why, with honey out of bare rock I would make you content.

Psalm 141

Psalm 141 implores the LORD's protection against the temptation to be tricky and to be seduced into living godlessly. *Don't empty out my life, LORD!* prays the psalmist, *but keep me focused on you, even if it takes the reproof of others who are more faithful than I am.*

A psalm of David

1 LORD God, I am crying to you — please, come to me quickly!
Do you not hear my voice when I call out to you?
2 My prayer is meant to be like an offering of good perfume
before your face.
My open palms raised in petition are to be like the
evening sacrifice of thanksgiving to you —

3 Set a guard before my mouth, O LORD God,
to keep watch before the door of my lips.
4 Please do not ever let my heart long for what is wicked,
for busying myself with the abuse of underhanded stuff,
working with people who practice what is cleverly evil —
don't let me eat their sweets!

5 When a tried-and-true right-doing person sharply corrects me,
it is like covenantal grace;
when such a trustworthy fellow calls me to account,
it is like an anointing oil — it will not be a blow to my head!
Yes, so long as such reproof happens,
my prayer too will hold up against the crookednesses
of the wicked.
6 When evildoers are dropped into the unforgiving hands
of their judges,
they may hear for the first time how sound my speaking
really was —
7 too late to stop their bones from being strewn in front
of the grave
like refuse and debris in the earth.

8 My eyes, however, are focused on you, LORD God,
  my LORD, I run to you for refuge — don't empty out my life!
9 Protect me from the hands of those who, tricky, lay a snare
          for me;
  secure me from the bait of those who practice evil deceit.
10 Let the godless all together fall into their own traps!
  while I myself escape safely. . . .

Psalm 141 (Versification)

I am crying, LORD, please come quickly!
Did you not hear my spoken prayer?
I deeply yearn to know you care.
My lifted hands still bring thanksgiving —

Guard my lips from mouthing words twisted.
Stop my enjoying sin as sweet.
LORD, strip my deeds of sly deceit.
Keep my poor heart from turning wicked.

When a trusted person corrects me,
I know the hurt brings healing grace.
How sad when judgment is not faced
until one's crooked life is wasted.

Your concern and power amaze me:
LORD, do not empty out my life!
Frustrate each wily tempter's vice —
let me walk past their traps in safety.

Tune: GENEVAN 141 (Genevan Psalter, 1562 edition)

Judges 5

Judges 5 is the stirring song of the brave Deborah, who excitedly recounts how the LORD God stirred some of God's people to consecrate themselves so thoroughly, despite the cowardice of other people of God, that they could let the LORD fight God's enemies for them. The enemies of God's people were crushed. May those who love you, LORD, rise and shine as the sun does in its splendor!

1 On that day Deborah sang a song, Barak the son of Abinoam too.
   This is the song:
2 For the fact that heads of hair in Israel hung wild and loose,
         and that the people gave themselves as freewill offerings:
   praise the LORD!
3 Listen, you kings! open your ears, you high officials!
   I am going to sing to the LORD God, I am,
   I'll sing and play my guitar for the LORD, the God of Israel!

[Flashback]

4 O LORD, when you formed a procession to move out of Seir,
   when you came up out of the open field country of Edom,
   the very earth shook;
   the skies seemed to spill, dark clouds spilled water down,
5 whole mountain ranges quaked back and forth in your presence,
         O LORD —
   it was all like Sinai in the presence of YAHWEH, God of Israel!

[Another flashback]

6 In the days of Shamgar Anath-son, in the days of Jael,
   caravans ceased to move through the land,
   and travelers who used highways trudged instead on winding
         back roads;
7 country farm folk no longer existed,
   country farm folk became extinct in Israel!

until I, Deborah, stood up,
until I boldly stood up, a mother in Israel!

8 People chose new-fangled gods:
that's why there were fights in the city gates!
And you didn't see shield nor spear among 40,000 men
in Israel. . . .
9 My heart goes out to the commanding officers of Israel
who gave themselves as freewill offerings among the people —
praise the Lord!

[Singing to people now, years later, after Judges 4 happened]

10 You who ride now on tan-colored she-asses,
you who sit on mats before the tent or openly walk the streets,
make these things known!
11 Above the noise of those who sound off at the watering holes,
there tell about the tried-tested-and-true reliability
of the Lord God,
the total reliability of the Lord for God's country farm folk
in Israel.

[Now comes a poetic account of what Judges 4 reports]

— Already the people of the Lord are storming to the city gates:
12 "Wake up, wake up, Deborah!
Wake up, wake up, sing out a song!
Get up, Barak! son of Abinoam,
go capture those who hold you captive!"
13 So, then finally a remnant stood up to the strong-armed ones;
the people of the Lord assembled before me surrounded
by hostile warriors:

[Deborah sings about the lineup of tribes, the provinces who came to fight]

14 You came from Ephraim — one of their roots, *Joshua*,
conquered — Amalek;

after you came Benjamin with all your kind;
commanding officers trooped up from Manasseh,
and from Zebulun came scouts who carried standards.
15 Chiefs in Issachar stood firm with Deborah;
like Issachar, so did the tribe of Barak — Napthali:
the massed company was set loose following him in the valley.

16 — Why did you just sit down there between the saddlebags
to listen so intently to the bleatings of the sheepies?!
O, in the territories of Reuben they had tremendous
heart-searching discussions:
17 Gilead too — the tribe of Gad — sat it out on the other side
of the Jordan,
and Dan, you were so busy, right? taking care of your
ship business. . . .
Asher sat around on its seashores, you took it easy
on your beaches, didn't you?
18 But Zebulun is a folk that scorns to save its life in the face
of death;
Napthali too fought almost recklessly on the heights
of open field country —

[Account of the battle]

19 Kings came, kings fought;
I tell you the kings of Canaan fought at Taanach by the waters
of Megiddo:
but they didn't pocket any silver booty.
20 The stars put up a fight right from heaven, shooting stars
battled with Sisera!
21 River Kishon washed the enemies away,
a running river of smashing turbulence — that's the river Kishon!
O my soul! march on, march on in triumph!
22 Yes, the battle horses' hoofs thundered on the ground
with galloping, galloping, the enemy stallions galloping
strong —
23 "Cursed be Meroz!" said the Angel of the LORD;

"Damn its inhabitants! May they be cursed,
because they did not come to the help of the Lord God!
They did not offer succor to the Lord amid all those
valiant fighters."

24 Blessed beyond all other women are you, Jael, wife of the
Kenite Heber!
Blessed are you among tent-women indeed!
25 Sisera begged for water: Jael gave him milk.
In a bowl fit for heroes she tendered him cream!
26 Her left hand crept out to get hold of the sturdy tent-pin;
her right hand reached for the heavy workman's hammer,
and she hammered Sisera down! She smashed his head;
she split, cracked his temples to pieces.
27 He slumped, fell, lay still between her feet.
Beneath her feet he slumped and fell down.
Where he had sunk there he lay fallen, devastated.

28 The mother of Sisera was on the lookout at the window;
busy peering through the shutters she complained,
"What in the world delays his chariot from coming?
What in the world detains the hoofbeats belonging
to his chariots?"
29 Her most astute princess waiting ladies give her an answer;
she really gives her reply to herself:
30 "They are finding, of course, and divvying up the spoil!
One girl's belly, two girls' bellies per soldier head!
Booty of richly dyed garments for Sisera!
Booty of clothings, embroidered garments richly colored
to adorn my neck — spoil! — "

31 So may all your enemies perish, O Lord God!
And may all those who love you rise and shine as the sun does
in its splendor!
And the land had it peaceful for forty years.

Isaiah 11

Isaiah 11 sings about the One who is coming — the shoot sprouting from the stump of Jesse — whom the Spirit of the LORD God shall invest with wisdom, God-fearing strength, and the insight to rule justly, ending violence. Then even animals will live peaceably together, and children shall be safe. Nothing evil will happen anymore, and the holy glory of the LORD shall fill the earth as water waves cover the sea.

1 There shoots a sprout out of the stump of Jesse!
  A new growth out of the old roots, and it will bear fruit!

2 The Spirit of the LORD God shall rest upon him:
  the spirit of wisdom and insight,
  the spirit of considered counsel and restful strength,
  a knowing spirit;
  a spirit of fearing the LORD God shall settle down upon him.
3 And he will be just glad to be fearing the LORD God!

  He shall not judge by what his eyes can see,
  and shall never decide a matter on what his ears hear.
4 No, he shall rule the cowering, defenseless ones protectively
  and speak law, judge with fairness for the poor hurt ones
          of the land.
  He shall stop dead in their tracks, by the blow of his mouth,
          the ruthless violent ones,
  and kill off the wicked by the breath of his lips.

5 So, right-dealing fits snug to his loins like a girdle, and
  trustworthy faithfulness clings to his hips like tights.

6 Then strangely,
  wolf will become guest at the lamb's,
  and leopard will lie down next to the kid goat;
  calf and sinewy young lion and choice fat cattle
  all together will be tended by a little boy;

7 the heifer and bear will associate peacefully
  and their young shall gambol together;
  lions shall eat pieces of straw like oxen —
8 And a breast-fed baby shall be able to drool and goo right
         on top of a poisonous snake's hole;
  a weaned child shall be able to stretch out its little hands
         to a nest of vipers:

9 nothing evil shall happen anymore!
  There will be no damaging, ruining, taking place anymore
         in all the strongholds of my holiness! says the LORD,
  because knowledge of the LORD God shall fill the earth
  like the water waves cover the sea!

10 And on that Day, the stump of Jesse, which had been standing
         around only as a warning sign to peoples of the earth:
  on that Day, unbelievers will look it up, turn to the root
         of Jesse questioningly listening —
  and the places where the One coming lodges
  shall be a stunning glory.

Isaiah 11:1-10 (Versification)

From Jesse's old stump a shoot will spring out:
like fruit from the root, a new branch will sprout.
God's Spirit will bless him with wisdom and might,
and awe for the LORD shall provide his delight.

He never shall judge by hearsay or sight.
His justice protects the poor in their plight.
The breath of his mouth stops the ruthless and cruel:
trustworthy, sure mercy shall clothe his new rule.

Then wolf with the lamb, the lion and calf,
the leopard with goat, shall gambol and laugh:
together the heifers and bears shall be guests,
and babies shall play near old poisonous nests.

Since knowledge of God shall cover the earth,
no creature shall hurt, destroy what has worth.
The nations shall seek him: their warfare shall cease,
and Jesse's new fruit shall bring glorious peace!

> Tune: GABRIEL'S MESSAGE (Basque carol,
> adapted by Edgar Pettmann)

9 *Hallelujah!*

Happy hours are good times to hallelu Yahweh
in the company of the faithful.

To sing *Hallelujah!* is tricky, since praise must be genuine, the real article, in its spontaneity. Otherwise we may be using the LORD's Name in vain.

Biblical warnings are severe against cheap praise, celebrations of our enthusiasm pitched like ritualistic sacrifices or thoughtless extravaganzas to impress God and others (Amos 5:21-24; Isaiah 1:10-20; Ecclesiastes 7:2-4). The praise the psalms practice and commend is focused on something specific — for example, thanking the LORD for God's incredible compassion in not dealing with us according to our sins (Psalm 103:8-18). Acceptable human praise is never just praise in general, but is always a happy doxological response to God's particular blessings, as in Hannah's and Mary's magnificats for the LORD's gift of a child (I Samuel 2:1-10; Luke 1:46-55) or the shouts of joy from the returned Babylonian exiles (Psalm 126).

Praise solid enough for the LORD to be enthroned upon (Psalm 22:3) has the heft of coming from lips which have historically walked with God through thick and thin; solid praise will be sensitive to the fact that others may be weeping, yet is glad to raise the brimful cup of Psalm 23 and toast God, "Cheers for the LORD" (Psalm 116:12-14)!

We humans need to keep in mind that praising the LORD is the regular purpose of all creatures. So exuberant paeans like Miriam's and Deborah's praise for the LORD's victory over enemies (Exodus 15:20-21; Judges 5) and our own dancing thanksgiving for being healed from cancer or given extra vigor in old age by the LORD's Spirit (Psalms 30:11-12; 92:10), join in with the ecstatic praise continually being offered up to the LORD by trees and flowers, sunshine and rain, angels, dragons, and snakes, as well as monarchs and generals of the world (Psalms 104; 148:7-10). Praise clamors to be a collective voice, a chorus. So that we humans, who know better than beasts and mountains the worth of reaching ends to endeavors, are not left behind by other creatural praise, Jesus taught us to pray, "Hallowed, honored as truly holy be your Name, O Lord!" To join the lightning and thunder and earthquake tremors in their praise of God, we should indeed pull out all the stops with flutes and drums, tubas, strings, woodwinds, trumpets, trombones, human voice, and dance to make a merry, raucous noise for the LORD (Psalm 150).

Psalm 103

Psalm 103 celebrates richly the tender, forbearing mercies of the LORD who does not deal with us according to our sins. As far as East is from West, so far God removes from us our dirty deeds. The LORD knows we are feeble earthlings, but remains faithful to generations of those who remember to do God's will. Along with all the angels, let all of me too praise the LORD!

In the line of David

1 Let me praise the LORD!
   Let everything deep inside me praise God's holy name!
2 Let me praise the LORD and not neglect, forget all the times
         God has come through — the LORD God!
3 who mercifully forgives all of a man or woman's guilt,
   who heals you in all your weaknesses,
4 keeps your life safe from the grave!
   who puts wreaths of long-range promises and gentle love
         around your neck,
5 who quiets your deep desires again and again with good things
   so that the young strength in you is quickened to soar
         like an eagle!

6 The LORD God is One who does what is right:
   God brings recompense to each one hurt unjustly.
7 God showed Moses what God was doing;
   God revealed to the children of Israel how God governs things:
8 compassionate, full of grace! is the LORD God,
   forbearing, rich in covenanting love.
9 It's true God does not plead with us forever;
   God does not hold back anger forever;
10 but the LORD does not deal with us according to our sins!
   God does not punish us to meet our guilt!

11 As the heavens arch over the earth,
   so God's engaging love covers those who fear the LORD.

12 As distant the East is from West,
   so far away does the LORD remove our dirty deeds from us.
13 As a father or mother lovingly accept their children,
   the LORD God accepts tenderly those who stand in awe of God,
14 for God knows what kind of creatures we are,
   God remembers we are earth,
15 that the days of a man or a woman are like grass,
   that a man or woman blossoms and blooms like a wild flower
16 which is gone when a hot wind blows over it
   and even the place where it stood forgets it was there.
17 But the love of our LORD God remains faithful forever and ever
      and ever to those who seek God.
18 The LORD God's steadfast, righteous mercy holds good
      for the children's children of those who keep God's
      covenanting bond, who keep on remembering God's
      Words by doing them.

19 Heaven is where the LORD God has established God's throne,
   But God's royal power stretches out and governs all things.

20 All angels, you strong fighters who do what God says,
      praise the LORD!
21 All God's fighting servants, you ministering ones doing
      what God wants, praise the LORD!
22 All God's creatures in all the places of God's provident rule,
      praise the LORD!
   Let all of me too praise the LORD!

Psalm 126

Psalm 126 savors the happy restoration of God's people after their being released unexpectedly from captivity. Flood our lives now, O LORD, with good beginnings! Those who sow in tears shall reap with joy.

A song to sing while walking up to Jerusalem

1 When the LORD brought back those of Zion left over
       from captivity,
  why we were like people in a dream —
2 mouth filling up with laughter, bubbling over happily in speech.
  Then even the unbelievers were saying,
  "The LORD has done great things for them!"
3 Yes, the LORD has done great things with us.
  That is why we are so glad.

4 LORD, please turn around to good our unexpected return,
  just as you let loose the swollen streams in the South.

5 Those who sow in tears shall reap with joy.
6 Whoever goes out crying, goes out carrying live seed,
  will come back — no doubt about it — come back triumphantly
  carrying bundles of grain.

Psalm 126 (Versification)

When God brought Zion's remnant band back to the land,
we felt like we were dreaming.
Why, even unbelievers said, "The LORD has led
with mighty works, redeeming."
Come, laugh for joy! our songs employ —
the LORD has won, great things begun,
has filled our lives with meaning!

Please bless our new beginnings, LORD, as you refilled
the Negev's dried out basin;
so those who suffered sowing seed will now be freed
to reap with deep elation.
Who sows with tears, but perseveres,
comes home again with sheaves of grain,
surprised by God's salvation.

Tune: MAG ICH UNGLUCK (J. Klug's *Geistliche Lieder*, 1535)

Psalm 148

Psalm 148 enjoins all creation — angels, moons, oceans, whirlpools, wild and domestic animals, even snakes — to exult in the LORD God who ordained their wondrous creaturely praise. And let world rulers, youth, the elderly, and any children also hallelu the LORD who shoulders the weakness of God's people, those who stay close to the LORD.

Cantor:

1 Hallelu Yahweh!
  Hallelu Yahweh all the way down from heaven
  and all the way back!
2 All angels — all God's veteran angels, hallelu Yahweh!
3 Sun and moon, hallelu Yahweh!
  Every star alight, hallelu Yahweh!
4 Endless end of the sky and hidden reach of the oceans,
  hallelu Yahweh!

Congregated faithful:

5 They shall hallelu the name of the LORD,
  for the LORD commanded, and they were created.
6 God set them up forever.
  God made them an ordinance which they do not overstep.

Cantor:

7 Hallelu Yahweh, every crack in the earth!
  All you dragons, whirlpools, and burning fires,
8 hail, snow, and smoke,
  wind wedded to the storm blowing where God speaks,
9 you mountain and little hills everywhere,
  fruit trees and all cedars,
10 all wild animals, all animals near the house,
  you snakes and birds on the wing:

Congregated faithful:

Hallelu the name of the LORD!

Cantor:

11 Rulers and judges on the earth, every nation,
12 you young fellows, you young women,
    the older ones with gray in the hair, and any children:
13 let them hallelu the name of Yahweh,
    because only God's name is to be praised.
    God's glory soars beyond earth and heaven itself.

14 The LORD God will shoulder the weakness of God's people.
    And the LORD shall shore up praise for all God's lowly
            faithful ones,
    for the sons and daughters of Israel,
    the folk that stay close to the LORD.

Congregated faithful:

Hallelujah!

Psalm 150

Psalm 150 is a hallelujah chorus of brass instruments, strings, tympany, flutes, and cymbals making a joyful noise to celebrate God's grand, sovereign Rule in heaven and on earth. Let every thing that has a breath hallelu the LORD God!

1 Hallelu YAHWEH!

Hallelu the LORD in God's holy place!
Hallelu the LORD through the heavens God rules!
2 Hallelu the LORD for God's sovereignty!
Hallelu the LORD in the overwhelmingness of God's grandeur!

3 Hallelu YAHWEH with the blast of trumpet!
Hallelu YAHWEH with harps and bass violins!
4 Hallelu YAHWEH with bouncing tambourines and dance!
Hallelu YAHWEH with stringed instruments, with flutes!
5 Hallelu YAHWEH with ringing cymbals!
Hallelu YAHWEH with big cymbals crashing joyfully!

6 Let every thing that has a breath hallelu the LORD God!

HalleluJAH!

Psalm 150 (Versification)

Hallelu the LORD our God!
Praise God in God's holy place.
Praise God in the skies God rules.
Praise God for God's sovereignty.
Praise God's overwhelming grandeur!
Every creature far and near,
make your joyful noise and cheer:
honor, glory, praise the LORD God!

Praise God with the trumpet blast!
Crash your cymbals, laugh with dance!
Praise with flute, with drums and strings!
Every creature that has breath,
celebrate until the earth rings:
Hallelu the great I AM!
Hallelu the worthy Lamb!
Hallelu the LORD our Savior!

Tune: GENEVAN 150 (Genevan Psalter, 1551 edition)

A Congregational Paean
(Versification)

When a follower of the LORD in poor health is suddenly healed, when an arduous task is finally finished, when a person becomes happily remarried, or is released from being an imprisoned hostage, God's Word of the psalms says, "Cheer God's mysterious ways and celebrate the LORD's glory!"

The Genevan melody of Psalm 89 has the lift-off, syncopated rhythmic character and tensile strength of serious merriment: gratefulness, mystery, and jubilee sparkle through its long, joyful, wiry melodic lines. The LORD redeems the weak — us failures — and amazingly re-creates our frustrated lives. Hear our excited shouts, LORD, spirits now are buoyant! Your simple miracle turns trouble into triumph — Hallelujah!

1*

How shall we thank you, LORD, for joy and this surprise?
You have come through again to re-create our lives.
We stand amazed: your providential hand looks after
our struggling daily cares; your kiss fills mouths with laughter.
Hear our excited shouts, LORD, spirits now are buoyant.
Your simple miracle turns trouble into triumph.

2 [For *unexpected healing*]

How good it is to see your healing touch of health
restore [**'s] blood and breath to normal life's prime wealth.
Gone is the pain, the doubts, †his feeling unprotected:

---

*   Stanza 1 usually is sung first. Then the congregation sings the stanza appropriate for the occasion.

** Insert the name of the one who is intended for commemoration.

†   Use his/her/their or brother/sister/members as appropriate.

You wiped away the tears when suffering was expected —
praised be your Name, O LORD, you have redeemed †his story!
We cheer your mystery and celebrate your glory.

3 *[For completion of a difficult task]*

How good it is to have all toilsome tension past.
You have supplied a fruitful finish now at last.
Struggles and setbacks plagued the arduous undertaking,
but you ordained the outcome far beyond our making —
praised be your Name, O LORD, you have redeemed †her story!
We cheer your mystery and celebrate your glory.

4 *[For a late marriage or remarriage in the LORD]*

How good it is to know your grace fills out one's life
from solitary walk to wedded husband-wife.
Intimacy and passion joined by love are gifted
by you, O God, with double power and joy committed —
praised be your Name, O LORD, you have redeemed their story!
We cheer your mystery and celebrate your glory.

5 *[For release of captive or hostage]*

How good it is to see our †brother face to face,
brought back from exile sound, kept safe by your embrace.
Captivity is cruel and breaks the best communion:
God, swallow up our loss; begin with this reunion —
praised be your Name, O LORD, you have redeemed our story!
We cheer your mystery and celebrate your glory.

6 [For other special festive events, or use as final stanza]

How good it is to taste exultant jubilee!
You feed us from the honeycomb, and make us free.
Your generosity provides more than requested:
teach us to dance and sing, your children glad and festive —
praised be your name, O Lord, you have redeemed our story!
We cheer your mystery and celebrate your glory.

Tune: GENEVAN 89 (Genevan Psalter, 1551 edition)

A Concluding Word:
The Psalms for Worship

In the last generation in various communions throughout the world, there has been renewed interest in psalmody and in producing complete psalters. The Pontifical Biblical Institute published a new Latin *Psalter* in 1945 for priests to use for their daily offices. French Catholics behind *Le Bible de Jérusalem* — Tournay, Schwab, Chillot, and Joseph Gelineau — promoted rhythmic chanting of the *Psalms* in the 1950s. Reformation churches in the Netherlands produced a new versified psalter to Genevan melodies, along with hundreds of hymns with fresh tunes, in the widely used *Liedboek voor de Kerken* (1953-1968). During the 1960s British Anglicans rallied with new tunes as well as new texts in *Psalm Praise* (1973), although they did not publish a complete psalter in English.

Updated versifications for all 150 Genevan melodies are found in the Canadian Reformed *Book of Praise, Anglo-Genevan Psalter* (developed 1972-1984). The Christian Reformed Church's *Psalter Hymnal* (1977-1987) holds all 150 psalms in metrical versions for congregational singing with melodies from various confessional traditions and from different centuries of composition. The Reformed Presbyterian Church in North America still sings only psalms in worship services, unaccompanied, as found in their complete metrical psalter, *The Book of Psalms for Singing* (1973). That edition is the latest of their revisions that still perpetuate the antiquated language and syntax of the old Scottish Psalters. There is a carefully phrased Roman Catholic liturgical version of *The Psalter* for reciting the psalms communally (1980-1994). The Canadian Presbyterian Church has produced *The Book of Psalms* (1986-1995), which provides a mix of texts and tunes for responsorial use. A complete psalter is included in the South African *Liedboek van die Kerk* (1986-2001). Genevan melodies of the psalms are being given vigorous attention in the Hungarian and Japanese languages. Reformed churches in Japan have just completed versification of all 150 psalms in Japanese, to be sung to the Genevan tunes (published in installments like the original Genevan Psalter). Reformed churches in Hungary have kept the complete Genevan Psalter in their psalter hymnals to this day.

But congregational practice in North America is not so enthusiastic and rigorous as such leadership might hope. The practice of singing psalms to deepen the confession and worship of the congregated faithful is spotty. This little book, with its CD, wishes to encourage, in its own way, the use of psalms as an integral part of liturgical preparation and response to the preaching of God's word.

Past service of psalms in worship

The contested history of dating and locating the psalms, and determining their original use, is not our concern here. That King David gave professional status to psalm writers and musicians is certain (I Chronicles 15–16 and 23). That recitation of litanies and the sounding of trumpets and musical instruments were normal on festive days and in connection with processions and choreographed dances near the altar in the first and the second Jerusalem temples is also documented in Scripture (I Kings 8; II Chronicles 29; cf. Psalm 43:3-4). That Jesus quoted the psalms (Psalms 22, 31, 69, and 110) and that the Newer Testament is replete with references to all manner of psalms (Acts 4:23-31 on Psalm 2, Hebrews 3:1–8:1 on Psalms 95 and 110) indicates the relevance of the Older First Testament of Psalms for "the last days" (I Peter 1:13-21; II Peter 3:1-7), in which we are historically alive today.

Because the biblical psalms have God speaking to us through the daily vicissitudes of faithful people, there is a broad scope to the psalms' conception of serving the LORD. The psalms assume that a person serves the LORD also outside the temple, without the bloody sacrifices of livestock or the roasting of grain.

The psalmists themselves practice serving the LORD in their wise reflection (Psalms 1, 2, 19, 39, and 56; Ecclesiastes 3:1-15), in commenting on historical events (Psalms 78, 81, and 126; Judges 5; I Samuel 2:1-10), and in making intercession for those suffering injustice (Psalms 34, 86, and 110).

Some of the psalms do seem expressly intended to be celebrations before the LORD in the temple precincts (Psalms 30, 89, 115, 141, 148, 150). Other psalms are deeply personal confessions which are incorporated by the leading of God's Spirit into shared liturgical services (Psalms 32, 51, and 130). Most psalms have various facets to their makeup and so are multipurpose, adaptable, and appropriate for different settings.

In earlier days of the church, the psalms were a staple in the diet of Christ's followers. It was part of the Rule of Saint Benedict (c. 530) that Benedictine monks were to recite during the day and the night in the monastery all 150 psalms each week; additional psalm recitations could be required for rites of penance. Around the time of the Council of Trent (1545-1563), it was prescribed that all clerics should take time for the same monastic practice, about 21 psalms per day and night, principally to focus meditation on the doctrinal instruction the psalms provided. Only at the Second Vatican Council (1962-1965) was this weekly regimen for priests relaxed; now a priest is expected to recite almost all the psalms once a month. (Such a habit of reading the psalms has long been recommended for those who use the psalm texts found in the Anglican *Book of Common Prayer*.)

Integral to the Reformation in Europe was Martin Luther's proposal that "the whole Psalter, psalm by psalm, should remain in use" and that the congregation should hear "entire psalms" in worship services in their vernacular language. Also critical for the thrust of the Reformation was John Calvin's persistence in producing a complete French Psalter with gifted poets Clement Marot and Theodor Beza and with quality composers like Matthias Greiter and Louis Bourgeois, so God's illiterate people could voice God's psalms in church worship services and also sing them at home, at school, and in workplaces.

The Genevan Psalter (released in installments from 1539 to 1562) was translated into Dutch verse by Petrus Dathenus (1566), so the Genevan Psalms were firmly situated early in the Reformed Church liturgies of the Netherlands (synodically authorized in 1568 and not revised until 1773). The Genevan Psalter spread quickly also to other lands by being translated into 24 languages — for example, by Ambrosius Lobwasser into German (1573) and by Albert Szenci Molnar into Hungarian (1607).

Particularly noteworthy is the dissemination of the Genevan Psalter into English-speaking lands by way of the Protestants who fled for their lives from England to Frankfurt, Strasbourg, and Geneva during the reign of Mary Tudor (1553-1558) and then later returned during Queen Elizabeth I's reign (1558-1603), bringing with them a fresh English translation of the Bible (The Breeches Bible, 1560) and an interest to update *The Certayne Psalms,* which had been put into the meter of English ballads earlier by Thomas Sternhold (c. 1549).

John Knox oversaw an expanded edition of Sternhold in Geneva (1556), completed in 1564 in Scotland. In 1562 all 150 psalms, completed mostly by John Hopkins, were published in London by John Day. Those psalters became the songbook of Scottish Presbyterian and English Anglican communions. The settings with short tetrameter-trimeter rhymed lines (particularly three meters now known as common, long, and short meters) became the standard for singing psalms. By the time the text was officially revised in 1696 by Nahum Tate and Nicholas Brady, with the imprimatur of the king, only texts of the psalms were printed, appended in the back of the Book of Common Prayer, because most psalms were sung to just three or four well-known common or long meter tunes.

Psalms also reached the "New World." A Huguenot refugee colony in Florida (1562-1565) brought from Europe their Genevan psalter and taught local Indians the melodies (see Charles Baird, "Introduction" to *History of the Huguenot Emigration to America* [New York: Dodd, Mead, 1885], especially 1:36-42; 65–68; 99–103). The Pilgrims who founded the colony at Plymouth Rock in 1620 used *The Book of Psalmes Englished both in Prose and Metre* by Henry Ainsworth (published in Amsterdam, 1612), which contained a goodly number of melodies from the Franco-Dutch psalter. The Puritans who founded the Massachusetts Bay colony in 1629 imported the Sternhold and Hopkins *Psalter,* but soon revised the texts to be more biblically literal and reduced the number of common meter tunes to be used. The resultant "Bay Psalm Book," *The Whole Booke of Psalmes Faithfully Translated into English* (1640), became the main songbook for churches in the Colonies for almost 100 years.

In New York the Dutch colonial church used the Dathenus Genevan Psalter prescribed by the Synod of Dordt (1648) until 1767, when Francis

Hopkinson translated the texts into English and adapted Tate and Brady psalm versions to fit the Genevan melodies. So for centuries psalms are what were sung by believers in English-speaking Protestant churches.

But psalms were gradually overtaken in England by hymns around the time of Isaac Watts. Watts's great hymn "Joy to the World," a paraphrase of Psalm 98, was published in 1707, and Watts brokered the change from psalms to hymns with *Psalms of David imitated in the Language of the New Testament and applied to the Christian State and Worship* (1719). Hundreds of hymns were bound together with these psalm paraphrases. Charles (1707-1788) and Samuel (1810-1876) Wesley made hymns the trademark of Protestant evangelical Methodist church members. In the British Victorian period, when the Anglican communion was the established confession and the organ was king, great stately hymns were written for an educated, literate populace who were led by trained choirs in vespers and worship services. Psalm-singing gradually became rare in mainstream communions.

In the United States of America, hymns also came to overwhelm psalm-singing, especially after the post-Revolutionary "Second Great Awakening" (c. 1795-1830), when a voluntaristic Arminian theology and revivalism swept the country. Even reading psalms in a worship service became reduced to certain selected, favorite psalms. Often psalms were excerpted — a whole psalm often takes more time than an efficient liturgy can afford — thinning out the hard parts that seemed extravagant or pugnacious to the refined, middle-class sensibilities of pious democratic believers (like excising the curse in Psalm 139:19-22). Moreover, an evangelistic frontier camp meeting needs upbeat songs with refrains to hold people's attention!

On integrating biblical psalms liturgically
in church worship services

If one excerpts psalms for use, one tends to pull God's Word instrumentally down into our horizons rather than situate our perceived needs and desires into the setting of God's revealed psalmic horizon. However, believers may expect God's psalm setting to give a normative context and stretch to the problems of our daily life which we bring to congregational worship.

Since most whole psalms were not written to fit our orders of Christian worship and were not conceived to follow the lectionary celebration of Christ's birth, Lenten suffering, Easter, or Pentecost, one must be imaginative and circumspect in linking psalms, which have their own integrity, to a liturgical context, which also has its legitimate centers of concern.

One way to respect a psalm in worship is to take it in its entirety as the text for sermonic exposition, and then sink the message of the psalm into the congregation's experience by having them sing its versification.

Various psalms in this collection would be appropriate for specific steps in a worship service, as reading or as singing:

Opening of worship:	Psalms 8 (choral), 19, 115 (choral)
Confessions of sin:	Psalms 6, 32, 38, 51
Assurance of forgiveness:	Psalms 103, 130
Direction for life:	Psalms 86, 141
Prayer for illumination:	Psalm 1
Thanksgiving:	Psalms 148 (choral), 150
Eucharist:	Psalm 116
Benediction:	Psalm 91

A good way to reinforce a psalm in the churchgoer's consciousness is to both speak and sing the psalm. Also, if one were to repeat the psalm in the same liturgical spot for a month or two of Sundays, believers would gradually be able to own that psalm with familiarity. Especially when the choral reading of a psalm is effectively prepared, hearing and participating in it makes the psalm come alive existentially for those present.

Various psalms in this collection would be appropriate for speaking during particular stages of the church worship year. One can consult the *Revised Common Lectionary* (1992) to find which psalm fragments are used at given times; but if we try to keep the integrity of a whole psalm before us, the following psalms do well for certain occasions:

Advent:	Psalm 25; Isaiah 10:1-10
Christmas:	Psalms 8 (choral), 148 (choral)
Epiphany:	Psalms 19, 30, 62, 92
Lent:	Psalms 3 (choral), 5, 6, 13, 22, 32, 38, 51, 116, 130; Ecclesiastes 3:1-15

Easter:	Psalm 23; Jonah 2; Job 19
Ascension:	Psalms 2 (choral), 110; I Samuel 2:1-10
Pentecost:	Psalms 81, 90, 103
Christian Life:	Psalms 1, 34, 42–43, 56, 91, 126, 139, 141

For official liturgical scripture readings, some traditions insist on using only officially approved Bible translations. In these contexts, the versions presented in this volume may be especially useful in personal or group preparation for worship. They may also suggest metaphors, phrases, and images that could be used in the extemporaneous parts of liturgy — sermons, prayers, introductions. Some congregations may also be open to having these texts in various parts of the liturgy, such as a prayer of confession or blessing, while retaining official translations for the scripture readings that precede the sermon.

This *Voicing God's Psalms* book and CD is meant to be exploratory rather than complete, an encouraging pointer rather than a canonic model. That the versifications are partial to Genevan and Welsh melodies is not to be taken as if they were sacrosanct. The emphasis is an attempt to revive a rich treasure that has become obscured by antiquated texts, poor performance practice (sung too slowly), and having psalms refitted to oversimplified tunes. Instead of monodic chanted text (Gelineau) or a mix of speech and sung refrain (Presbyterian *Book of Psalms*), preference is indeed given here to metrical congregational psalm singing as a most rich public way to experience communal worship that has spillover into the devotional life of families, schools, other gatherings of believers, and one's own meditative devotions.

The Basque carol and the African American Blues melodies in this present collection suggest that any melody worthy of a psalm text can be used if its tonality deftly catches the embattled faith complexity of God's Word and does not shortchange the whole. The original African American Blues, akin to "Spirituals" and their pentatonic clutch of tones, certainly deserve a wider hearing connected with God's psalms because, like the biblical psalm laments, the early Blues (before their metamorphosis in "clubs" and electronification) are melodically steeped in the simple suffering of an "elect" community of believers, expositing the cry of so many biblical pleas. The Genevan, Reformation German, and Welsh melodies are favored because their rich contribution to the psalms has been forgotten or dislocated, since so many of God's children today are isolated in the present, without historical sense of the communion of the saints stretching back for centuries.

Difficulties to be overcome in worshipping with psalms

The psalms as public communal expressions of faith are not where many North American people of God feel at home. Otherwise the psalms would be more on our lips, bespeaking our hearts. It will not help much to insert token psalm pieces here and there in worship services to make "the prayerbook of the church" once again the idiom of our liturgical worship. It will take concerted pastoral and musical leadership on location to get the psalms heard in their gritty integrity again.

There are at least two requisites for the psalms to come alive in our worship services: (1) Our congregational leaders must come to dwell in the psalms because they love to hear God's voice speaking there to all who have ears to hear; and (2) followers of Christ must grow the mind of Christ which realizes that congregational worship is meant to vindicate the Lord's Name in God's world and society by deepening the confession of the gathered faithful, rather than be primarily the occasion for an evangelistic rally or to congratulate ourselves on our salvation.

(1) To make the shift from introverted celebrative praise and petitions for God to help private me stay afloat: to shift a worship service over to prayer that has an honest psalmodic fervor of thankfulness for blessings received, and pleas to save us who obey God from going derelict, we who worship must become "poor in spirit" (Psalm 102:1; Matthew 5:3-10). To be able to love God's psalms requires that you engage the world as if you could let it go completely, says the Bible: you ply your trade and employ what comes your way and you accept your lifetime as a pure gift which you hold only for a little while in trust (I Corinthians 7:29-31) — you don't possess a thing. The "poor in Spirit" never claim any rights, the way Pharisees do (Luke 18:9-14), so utterly God-dependent do you take your existence to be. Then one's praise and laments can be selfless offerings that are surrounded by a cloud of witnesses (Hebrews 11:1–12:2) and whose transparent joy in the Lord surpasses understanding (Philippians 4:4-7).

And (2) to convert worship services from being a stage to captivate ignorant seekers with the milk of the gospel, and to transform Sunday morning services from being cocoons of saved individuals enjoying themselves: to transform a worship service into an ark of safety and wisdom with doors open to seasoned believers, disbelievers, outcasts, hypocrites, as well as naive questioners, we "dispossessed" trustees in God's world need to be driven by the Holy Spirit of intercessory prayer. Intelligent intercession for the LORD God to act with God's Spirit and hosts of angels to succor those beset by Evil who are at their wits' end is the gateway to living within the matrix of the psalms. The psalms embody and exemplify intercessory prayer that "availeth much" (James 5:13-18).

Even if we be relatively well off, to bear the neighbors' burdens by importuning the LORD to be present for their protection and comfort is fulfilling the law of Christ, say the Scriptures (Galatians 5:25–6:2). Maybe we can hardly articulate the laments of Scripture in church because we do not really know who our "neighbor" is during the week and how to give neighbors ongoing redemptive direction. Therefore we find it difficult to distinguish rejoicing with joyful Hallelujahs (Luke 15:3-10) from merely entertaining ourselves with songs of success (Amos 5:21-24).

If congregated believers could be led into hearing the psalms at full voice, while the convicting proclamation of God's Word is taking place, so that our songs resonate with the psalms' bittersweet, sad merriment in the LORD's grace, there would be a reformation in the quality of our worship services. Not a revival hour, but a reformation of our awareness of God's presence, Christ's Rule in God's world, and the Holy Spirit's dynamic for disciplined, giveaway lives of love.

Psalm 100

A voice melody for gratefully making good on a vow

Let all the earth get out its noise to the LORD God!
All of you, minister to the LORD God with mirth!
Come before the face of the LORD with shouts of jubilation!

Let all of you show you experientially know
that only the LORD Yahweh is God.
The LORD God made us.
We belong to Yahweh, we are God's people, the sheep
     and goats of God's pasture.

Enter God's gates with promised thanksgiving!
Come into the courtyard of the LORD singing praise!
Give thanks to the LORD, extol God's Name!

For the LORD God is good.
The LORD God's covenantal love holds forever and ever and ever.
The LORD God's trustworthy faithfulness lasts for generation
     after generation . . . after generation. . . .

CD Track List

The Calvin Institute of Christian Worship and Eerdmans Publishing Company present *Voicing God's Psalms,* a selection of translations and versifications of biblical psalms and canticles by Calvin Seerveld, read by the author, along with melodies appropriate for psalm versifications. For additional information, resources, and recordings, visit the website of the Calvin Institute of Christian Worship at *www.calvin.edu/worship/seerveld.*

Reader:	Calvin Seerveld
Choral Readers:	Michael Page, Lorien Reese, Dianna Clinch, Noah Thomas
Recorder:	Calvin Stapert
Saxophone:	Greg Marsden

1. Introduction [0:39]

2. Psalm 1 [1:29]

3. *Melody for Psalm 8 (Genevan Psalter), recorder* [0:46]

4. Psalm 19 [3:26]

5. *Psalm 2, choral reading* [2:43]

6. Psalm 110 [2:08]

7. *Melody for Psalm 110 (Genevan Psalter), recorder* [0:43]

8. *Psalm 115, choral reading* [2:49]

9. Ecclesiastes 3:1-15 [2:50]

10. Psalm 22 [5:18]

11. *Melody for Psalm 22 (Welsh Tune), recorder* [0:39]

12. Psalm 51 [4:05]

13. *Melody for Psalm 51 (Genevan Psalter), recorder* [1:30]

14. Psalm 130 [1:34]

15. *Melody for Psalm 130 (German tune), recorder* [1:04]

16. Psalm 39 [3:41]

17. *Melody for Psalm 42/43 (Genevan Psalter), recorder* [1:09]

18. Psalm 139 [4:26]

19. Psalm 23 [1:46]

20. Psalm 56 [3:11]

21. *Melody for Psalm 56 (Blues 56), saxophone* [1:33]

22. *Melody for Psalm 62 (Genevan Psalter), recorder* [0:50]

23. Psalm 92 [3:07]

24. *Melody for Psalm 92 (Genevan Psalter), recorder* [0:43]

25. *Melody for Psalm 92 (Blues 92), saxophone* [1:27]

26. Psalm 116 [2:56]

27. *Melody for Jonah 2 (Welsh tune), recorder* [1:04]

28. *Melody for Hannah's Magnificat (Genevan Psalter 37), recorder* [1:00]

29. Psalm 141 [2:39]

30. *Melody for Psalm 141 (Genevan Psalter), recorder* [0:42]

31. *Melody for Isaiah 11:1-10 (Basque Carol), recorder* [0:50]

32. Psalm 126 [1:18]

33. *Melody for Psalm 126 (German tune), recorder* [1:18]

34. *Psalm 148, choral reading* [2:13]

35. *Melody for Psalm 150 (Genevan Psalter) with variations by Jacob Van Eyck (c. 1590-1657), recorder* [3:05]

36. *Melody for Psalm 89 (Genevan Psalter), recorder* [1:07]